The RETURN
of the
LORD
Jesus

The RETURN

of the

LORD
Jesus

R. A. Torrey

W
WHITAKER
HOUSE

Publisher's note:
This new edition from Whitaker House has been updated for the modern
reader. Words, expressions, and sentence structure have been revised for
clarity and readability.

All Scripture quotations are taken from the King James Version of the
Holy Bible.

The Return of the Lord Jesus

(previously published with the title *Jesus Is Coming for You*)

ISBN: 978-1-60374-568-0

Whitaker House
1030 Hunt Valley Circle
New Kensington, PA 15068
www.whitakerhouse.com

This book has been printed digitally and produced in a standard
specification in order to ensure its continuing availability.

CONTENTS

Chapter 1

A VITAL TRUTH

Ye turned to God from idols to serve the living and true God;
and to wait for his Son from heaven, whom he raised from the
dead, even Jesus, which delivered us from the wrath to come.
—1 Thessalonians 1:9–10

The truth about the Lord's return is our safeguard against all heresies, errors, and falsehoods. One error after another is arising to deceive, *"if it were possible, even the elect"* (Mark 13:22). However, the truth of the second coming of Christ, which is clearly revealed in God's Word, proves them all wrong. It is remarkable that all forms of error contradict the doctrine of Christ's second coming. It is equally remarkable that all these errors are overthrown by the truth revealed in the Scriptures.

The truth of our Lord's return is the most precious truth the Bible contains. It fills the heart of the believer with joy, and it clothes him with strength for the battle. Lifting him above the sorrows, fears, necessities, trials, ambitions, and greed of this world, it makes him more than a conqueror in all things.

Obviously, the second coming of Christ is important, for it is mentioned more times in the New Testament than there are chapters—318 times in the 260 chapters of the New Testament. This doctrine, according to someone who has made it his lifelong study, occupies one in every twenty-five verses from Matthew to Revelation. It also occupies a prominent place in the Old

Testament, for by far the majority of the predictions concerning Christ in the Old Testament are connected, not with His first coming to die as an atoning Savior, but with His second coming to rule as King.

Help for the Hurting Heart

The coming again of Jesus Christ is the one doctrine with which God commands us to comfort sorrowing saints. When death had begun to thin the ranks of the believers in Thessalonica, and hearts were aching over separation from those who had passed away, the apostle Paul wrote,

> *But I would not have you to be ignorant, brethren, concerning them which are asleep* [dead], *that ye sorrow not, even as others which have no hope. For if we believe that Jesus died and rose again, even so them also which sleep in Jesus will God bring with him. For this we say unto you by the word of the Lord, that we which are alive and remain unto the coming of the Lord shall not prevent* [precede] *them which are asleep. For the Lord himself shall descend from heaven with a shout, with the voice of the archangel, and with the trump of God: and the dead in Christ shall rise first: then we which are alive and remain shall be caught up together with them in the clouds, to meet the Lord in the air: and so shall we ever be with the Lord. Wherefore comfort one another with these words.*
>
> (1 Thessalonians 4:13–18)

Since "*these words*" have to do entirely with the second coming of Christ, it is evident that the one doctrine with which God commands us to comfort those sorrowing over the loss of loved ones is Christ's second coming. No other truth has such comfort for believers when they are called upon to pass through deep sorrow.

On many occasions when I have written to those who have lost, for a time, those they love, I have obeyed God's commandment and used the truth of our Lord's return to comfort them. Many have told me afterwards how full of comfort this truth has proven to be when everything else had failed.

In the Old Testament we find God, through His servant Isaiah, comforting the people of Israel in the time of their misery and desolation with the thought of the Lord's coming:

> *Comfort ye, comfort ye my people, saith your God….O Zion, that bringest good tidings, get thee up into the high mountain; O Jerusalem, that bringest good tidings, lift up thy voice with strength; lift it up, be not afraid; say unto the cities of Judah, Behold your God! Behold…his reward is with him, and his work before him.*   (Isaiah 40:1, 9–10)

The Brightest Hope

Over and over in the New Testament, the coming again of our Lord Jesus Christ and the events connected with His coming are held up as *"that blessed hope"* (Titus 2:13), as well as the eager desire of every true believer. In Titus 2:13 Paul said, *"Looking for that blessed hope, and the glorious appearing of the great God and our Saviour Jesus Christ."* And Peter said,

> *Seeing then that all these things shall be dissolved, what manner of persons ought ye to be in all holy conversation and godliness, looking for and hasting unto the coming of the day of God, wherein the heavens being on fire shall be dissolved, and the elements shall melt with fervent heat?* (2 Peter 3:11–12)

To the true believer, the coming again of Jesus Christ is not something to dread, but it is the brightest hope the future holds for us. It should be the object of our eager desire and longing anticipation. The last prayer in the Bible should also be the cry of every wise Christian heart: *"Amen. Even so, come, Lord Jesus"* (Revelation 22:20).

The Object of Scorn

However, while the return of our Lord is the blessed hope and eager desire of the true believer, it is the particular object of the hatred and ridicule of the mockers who follow after their own evil desires. Peter's prediction has come true:

> *Knowing this first, that there shall come in the last days scoffers, walking after their own lusts, and saying, Where is the promise of his coming? for since the fathers fell asleep, all things continue as they were from the beginning of the creation.*
>
> (2 Peter 3:3–4)

A worldly church and worldly Christians join with these mockers in their hatred of this truth. As a wife who is flirting with other men does not long for the return of her absent husband, so the faithless bride of Christ, who is flirting with the world, does not long for the return of her Lord. But, for the believer whose affections are all fixed upon Jesus Christ, the Word of God contains no other promise so precious as the promise that He is soon coming again. A person's attitude toward the coming again of Jesus Christ is a good indication of his spiritual state.

The Best Reason to Live Righteously

The fact that our Lord Jesus is coming again is the great biblical argument for a life of watchfulness, fidelity, wisdom, activity, simplicity, self-restraint, prayer, and abiding in Christ. During the last week of His earthly life, our Lord said to His disciples, *"Therefore be ye also ready: for in such an hour as ye think not the*

Son of man cometh" (Matthew 24:44). In our day we are constantly urging men to be ready because death may overtake them at any moment, but this was not the argument that our Lord Jesus used. It was His own coming, not the coming of death, that He held up before His disciples as the incentive to live as they ought to live.

Still speaking of His coming, Jesus said,

Who then is a faithful and wise servant, whom his lord hath made ruler over his household, to give them meat in due season? Blessed is that servant, whom his lord when he cometh shall find so doing.   (Matthew 24:45–46)

On another occasion, when our Lord was warning His disciples against the sins that are especially common in our day— overeating, overdrinking, and overconcern with the cares of this life—He said,

And take heed to yourselves, lest at any time your hearts be overcharged with surfeiting [overindulgence], and drunkenness, and cares of this life, and so that day come upon you unawares. For as a snare shall it come on all them that dwell on the face of the whole earth. Watch ye therefore, and pray always, that ye may be accounted worthy to escape all these things that shall come to pass, and to stand before the Son of man.   (Luke 21:34–36)

It was not the physical effects of overeating and overdrinking that our Lord held up as a warning to His disciples, but rather the fact that these things would make them ill-suited to meet Him at His return.

The apostle John wrote to those whom he had led into the light, *"Now, little children, abide in him; that, when he shall appear, we may have confidence, and not be ashamed before him at his coming"* (1 John 2:28). There are many reasons that we should abide in the

Lord Jesus, but the preeminent reason in John's mind was that Jesus is coming again. If we are to have confidence and not be ashamed before Him when He comes, we must be abiding in Him.

Watching for His Return

Our Lord Jesus told us that His return is the one event for which we should always be watching. He said,

> *Let your loins be girded about* [keep yourself dressed and ready], *and your lights burning; and ye yourselves like unto men that wait for their lord, when he will return from the wedding; that when he cometh and knocketh, they may open unto him immediately.* (Luke 12:35–36)

In the next verse a special blessing is pronounced upon those whom the Lord will find watching when He comes:

> *Blessed are those servants, whom the lord when he cometh shall find watching: verily I say unto you, that he shall gird himself, and make them to sit down to meat, and will come forth and serve them.* (verse 37)

The Holy Spirit told us in Hebrews 9:28 that *"unto them that look for him,"* Jesus will *"appear the second time without sin unto salvation."* These words ought to lead us into some very deep and earnest thinking and to ask ourselves whether we are really looking, watching, and waiting for Him.

My Own Encounter with This Crucial Truth

It is evident from what has been said in this chapter that the truth of our Lord's second coming is a truth of foremost importance.

Unfortunately, many consider the doctrine of the second coming of Christ to be an impractical doctrine. I once regarded it that way myself. In my early ministry, one of my church members came to me and asked if I would speak on the second coming of Christ. I knew nothing about the doctrine and put him off, thinking to myself, "This church member will be a much older man than he is now before I speak on a doctrine so impractical." But the day came when I found that it was not only one of the most precious, but also one of the most practical doctrines in the whole Bible.

There have been four marked epochs in my Christian experience. The first was when I came to know the Lord Jesus as my personal Savior and my Lord. The second was when I discovered that the Bible is indeed the inerrant Word of God, that its statements are absolutely reliable in every respect, and that everything any man ever needed to know is contained in this one Book. The third was when I learned that the baptism with the Holy Spirit is for the present day and I claimed it for myself. And the fourth was when I saw the truth of the second coming of Christ. This truth transformed my whole idea of life. It broke the power that the world and its ambitions had over me, and it filled my life with the most radiant optimism in even the most discouraging circumstances.

Chapter 2

SCRIPTURAL PROOF

He which testifieth these things saith, Surely I come quickly.
Amen. Even so, come, Lord Jesus.
—Revelation 22:20

Beyond the shadow of a doubt, our Lord Jesus is coming again. How do we know that? Because God tells us so in His Word over and over again in the most explicit and unmistakable terms.

Passages That Give Proof

For instance, on the night before His crucifixion, our Lord Jesus said the following in order to comfort His disciples, who were overwhelmed with the thought that He was about to leave them: *"If I go and prepare a place for you, I will come again, and receive you unto myself; that where I am, there ye may be also"* (John 14:3). The apostle Paul took up this promise of his Lord and wrote,

> For the Lord himself shall descend from heaven with a shout, with the voice of the archangel, and with the trump of God: and the dead in Christ shall rise first: then we which are alive and remain shall be caught up together with them in the clouds, to meet the Lord in the air: and so shall we ever be with the Lord. (1 Thessalonians 4:16–17)

The apostle Paul doubtless had the words of Christ in mind when he wrote this, for there are four things that Paul said that exactly correspond to four things that Christ said. First, Jesus said, "*I will come again*"; Paul said, "*The Lord himself shall descend from heaven.*" Second, Jesus said, "*I will…receive you unto myself*"; Paul said, "*We…shall be caught up…to meet the Lord.*" Third, Jesus said, "*That where I am, there ye may be also*"; Paul said, "*So shall we ever be with the Lord.*" Fourth, Jesus prefaced His words with, "*Let not your heart be troubled*" (John 14:1). Paul closed his passage on Christ's second coming by saying, "*Comfort one another with these words*" (1 Thessalonians 4:18). Therefore, we clearly see that Paul's words are an inspired commentary upon the promise of Jesus.

To further prove that God plainly states in His Word that Christ is coming again, I will take you to one of Paul's later epistles:

For our conversation [citizenship] *is in heaven; from whence also we look for the Saviour, the Lord Jesus Christ: who shall change our vile body, that it may be fashioned like unto his glorious body, according to the working whereby he is able even to subdue all things unto himself.* (Philippians 3:20–21)

In Hebrews 9:28 we also read this: "*So Christ was once offered to bear the sins of many; and unto them that look for him shall he appear the second time without sin unto salvation.*"

The apostle Peter, in urging the Jews to repent, said,

Repent ye therefore, and be converted, that your sins may be blotted out, when the times of refreshing shall come from the presence of the Lord; and he shall send Jesus Christ, which before was preached unto you: whom the heaven must receive until the times of restitution of all things, which God hath spoken by the mouth of all his holy prophets since the world began. (Acts 3:19–21)

All the passages quoted, as well as many others, assert in the most distinct and unambiguous terms that our Lord Jesus is coming again.

Incorrect Interpretations

There are those who would interpret at least some of these Scriptures as referring to the death of the believer, but the passages will not permit this interpretation. At the death of the believer, while our Lord Jesus may draw near, He does not come *"with a shout,"* or, *"with the voice of the archangel,"* or, *"with the trump of God"* (1 Thessalonians 4:16). At the death of the believer, those who are alive and left certainly are not caught up *"to meet the Lord in the air"* (verse 17).

Jesus Himself drew a plain contrast between the death of the believer and His own coming again. Speaking to Peter about the future of John, He said, *"If I will that he [John] tarry till I come, what is that to thee?"* (John 21:22). It is plain from the context that *"If I will that he tarry"* means, "If I wish that he remain alive." Now, if we say that Christ's coming is at the believer's death, then we get this nonsense: "If I wish that he remain alive until he die, what is that to you?" Of course, this is not what our Lord meant. What He meant, as is plainly indicated by the words in their context, is, "If I wish that he remain alive until My own personal return, what is that to you?"

There are others who say that the coming again described in the quoted passages was simply the coming of Christ when the Holy Spirit came. The coming of the Holy Spirit is doubtless, in a very real and important sense, a coming of Christ. We see this in the book of John, where Jesus said,

> *If ye love me, keep my commandments. And I will pray the Father, and he shall give you another Comforter, that he may*

abide with you for ever; even the Spirit of truth; whom the world cannot receive, because it seeth him not, neither knoweth him: but ye know him; for he dwelleth with you, and shall be in you. I will not leave you comfortless: I will come to you.... He that hath my commandments, and keepeth them, he it is that loveth me: and he that loveth me shall be loved of my Father, and I will love him, and will manifest myself to him. Judas saith unto him, not Iscariot, Lord, how is it that thou wilt manifest thyself unto us, and not unto the world? Jesus answered and said unto him, If a man love me, he will keep my words: and my Father will love him, and we will come unto him, and make our abode with him.

(John 14:15–18, 21–23)

It is plain from these words that the coming of the Holy Spirit is a coming of Jesus Christ, because it is the Spirit's work to reveal Christ to us and to form Christ in us. However, this coming of Christ is not that which is referred to in the passages considered in the first section of this chapter. This is evident from the fact that all those promises but one, John 14:3, were made after the coming of the Holy Spirit and pointed to a future event.

In addition, at the coming of the Holy Spirit, Jesus does not receive us unto Himself to be with Him; rather, He comes to be with us. (See John 14:18, 21, 23.) However, at His coming again mentioned in John 14:3 and 1 Thessalonians 4:16–17, He takes us to be with Him.

Furthermore, at the coming of the Spirit, Christ does not *"change our vile body, that it may be fashioned like unto his glorious body"* (Philippians 3:21). And at the coming of the Spirit, there is no trumpet of God, no shout, no resurrection, no rapture in the clouds. In other words, the coming of Christ at the coming of the Holy Spirit does not conform at all to the plain and explicit statements of Christ and the apostles concerning His second coming.

Many scholarly students of the Bible, whose opinions are well worth considering, take the coming again mentioned in the passages quoted earlier to be at the destruction of Jerusalem. There is an element of truth in this interpretation. The destruction of Jerusalem was, in an important sense, a precursor, a prophecy, and a type of the judgment of the end of this age; therefore, in Matthew 24 and Mark 13 the two events are described in connection with each other. But God's judgment on Jerusalem in the first century is certainly not the event referred to in the passages given in the opening of this chapter. At the destruction of Jerusalem, those who had died in Jesus were not raised; living believers were not caught up to meet the Lord in the air; the bodies of believers were not transformed. Furthermore, years after the destruction of Jerusalem, we find John still looking forward to the Lord's coming as an event still to occur in the future. (See Revelation 22:20.) Even the following words, to which we referred earlier in the chapter, were written years after the destruction of Jerusalem:

> *Jesus saith unto him, If I will that he tarry till I come, what is that to thee? follow thou me. Then went this saying abroad among the brethren, that that disciple should not die: yet Jesus said not unto him, He shall not die; but, If I will that he tarry till I come, what is that to thee?* (John 21:22–23)

None of these events mentioned, nor all of them put together, nor any other event that has occurred, fulfills the very plain, explicit, and definite predictions and promises of our Lord Jesus and His apostles regarding His coming again. The coming again of Jesus Christ, which is so frequently mentioned in the New Testament as the great hope of the church, is an event that still lies in the future.

Chapter 3

HOW WILL IT HAPPEN?

*And while they looked stedfastly toward heaven as he went up,
behold, two men stood by them in white apparel; which also
said, Ye men of Galilee, why stand ye gazing up into heaven?
this same Jesus, which is taken up from you into heaven, shall
so come in like manner as ye have seen him go into heaven.*
—Acts 1:10–11

The belief that our Lord Jesus is coming again is generally held by all who really believe in the Bible, but there is a wide diversity of opinion as to how He will come again. However, if we go to the Bible to find out what it teaches, instead of trying to read our own views into the Bible, there are many things about the manner of His coming that are perfectly plain.

In Person

First of all, it is perfectly plain that His coming will be personal. That is, His coming is not merely the coming of a great revival or a moral reformation or a social uplift; nor is it the disclosure of some new truth. It is the coming of our Lord Jesus Himself. In His promise to His disciples on the night of His crucifixion, He said, *"I will come again"* (John 14:3). And the context clearly shows that He meant that He personally will come. As we saw in the last chapter, the apostle Paul wrote, *"The Lord himself shall descend from heaven"* (1 Thessalonians 4:16).

Two men, who stood by the disciples as they watched Jesus ascend, said,

> *Ye men of Galilee, why stand ye gazing up into heaven? this same Jesus, which is taken up from you into heaven, shall so come in like manner as ye have seen him go into heaven.*
>
> (Acts 1:11)

There is no mistaking the meaning of these words. Jesus Himself, the same Jesus who went away, is coming back again.

A minister of the Gospel once wrote, "We must not expect a personal return of our Lord, but be satisfied with Him as coming more and more in all the wonders and glories of this closing nineteenth century." The man who wrote these words was seemingly a good and godly man, a man who had made great sacrifices for the Lord Jesus Christ, but I have never been able to comprehend how anyone who really loved the Lord could have written these words. The wonders and glories of the closing nineteenth century were beneficial enough, in their place, and for them we thank God; but if one really loves the Lord, it is not the wonders and glories that he longs for, but for Jesus Himself. As much as we rejoice in His works, it is He whom we long for. It is He whom we must have, and it is He whom we will have.

Suppose a bridegroom has left his bride and has gone into a distant land to prepare a home for her, assuring her that at the right time he himself will return to take her to her new home. Every now and then he has sent her some gift as a reminder and as a token of his continued love. One day a friend visits the bride and finds her eagerly looking forward to the day when the bridegroom himself will return for her. After listening to her speak of her longing for the return of her loved one, he says to her, "You must not expect a personal return of your husband. When he told you he would come again, he did not refer to his personal return. Has he not sent you many gifts as tokens of his love?" "Yes," she replies. "Well," he continues, "it is not for him that you must look; you must learn to be satisfied with his coming to you more and more in the gifts that he is sending you from time to time." What would the bride reply? She would answer, "I do not desire his gifts. I am longing for him."

Likewise, it is for Jesus Himself that the true believer is longing. We cannot be satisfied with His coming more and more in the richer experiences of grace that are constantly coming to us by the power of the Holy Spirit. We long for Him. We must have Him, and we will have Him. The same Jesus who was taken up into heaven will come back in the same way that He left.

Bodily and Visibly

The verses already quoted clarify a second thing about the second coming of our Lord; that is, He will come bodily and visibly. He *"shall so come in like manner"* (Acts 1:11) as He was seen going into heaven. By any fair interpretation, this can mean nothing short of a visible and bodily coming. It might mean more than that, but it cannot mean less.

Some have said that the expression *"so come in like manner"* only indicates the certainty of His coming and has nothing to do with the manner of His coming. However, the original Greek words of the verse do not allow this meaning. The literal translation of the original Greek is, "Thus will come in the manner which." This form of expression is never used anywhere to indicate mere certainty, but always to indicate manner. In the very manner in which the disciples saw Him go, He will come again. He went from their sight bodily and visibly. They *"looked stedfastly toward heaven as he went up"* (Acts 1:10), and we will see Him when He comes again.

Furthermore, in Hebrews 9:28 we read, "*So Christ was once offered to bear the sins of many; and unto them that look for him shall he appear the second time without sin unto salvation.*" The Greek word translated "*shall…appear*" literally means "shall be seen." The word has no other meaning but to be seen with the eyes.

If possible, this truth is even clearer in Revelation 1:7: "*Behold, he cometh with clouds; and every eye shall see him.*" Once, at the close of a sermon on the second coming of Christ, a skeptic approached me and asked, "You do not think, do you, that when Jesus comes again, He will actually be seen with the eyes?" I replied, "It does not matter what I think; the only question is, What does God's Word say? And God says distinctly in His Word, '*Behold, he cometh with clouds; and every eye shall see him.*'"

Of course, this statement does not fit in with the teaching of many current theories, but it is the plain teaching of the Word of God. It cannot be escaped, except by a manipulation of God's Word that would lead to utter confusion if applied to other passages. If the Bible teaches anything definitely and distinctly, it teaches that the Lord Jesus, who was taken up visibly and bodily from Mount Olivet into heaven in the sight of the disciples, is coming again visibly and bodily in our sight. We will not merely feel His spiritual presence near us; we will see Him as truly and as distinctly as the disciples saw Him when He stood talking with them on Mount Olivet the moment before His feet left this earth.

In Three Stages

There will be three different stages of this personal, visible coming of our Lord. The first stage of His coming will be when He comes in the air, where believers will be caught up to meet Him. This stage is described in a passage that I have already quoted, but it bears repeating:

For the Lord himself shall descend from heaven with a shout, with the voice of the archangel, and with the trump of God: and the dead in Christ shall rise first: then we which are alive and remain shall be caught up together with them in the clouds, to meet the Lord in the air: and so shall we ever be with the Lord. (1 Thessalonians 4:16–17)

The second stage will be when He comes to the earth. This stage is described in the following passages of Scripture:

When the Son of man shall come in his glory, and all the holy angels with him, then shall he sit upon the throne of his glory: and before him shall be gathered all nations: and he shall separate them one from another, as a shepherd divideth his sheep from the goats. (Matthew 25:31–32)

And his feet shall stand in that day upon the mount of Olives, which is before Jerusalem on the east, and the mount of Olives shall cleave in the midst thereof toward the east and toward the west, and there shall be a very great valley; and half of the mountain shall remove toward the north, and half of it toward the south. And ye shall flee to the valley of the mountains; for the valley of the mountains shall reach unto Azal: yea, ye shall flee, like as ye fled from before the earthquake in the days of Uzziah king of Judah: and the LORD my God shall come, and all the saints with thee. (Zechariah 14:4–5)

From the closing words of the latter passage, it is evident that in this second stage His saints will come with Him. This is also evident from 1 Thessalonians 3:13: *"To the end he may stablish your hearts unblameable in holiness before God, even our Father, at the coming of our Lord Jesus Christ with all his saints,"* and 1 Thessalonians 4:14: *"For if we believe that Jesus died and rose again, even so them also which sleep in Jesus will God bring with him."* In the air our Lord comes for His own, and to the earth He comes with His own.

For all that we know, a considerable interval may take place between the first and second stages of the Lord's coming. Two passages of Scripture seem to hint that the Great Tribulation takes place between the coming of Jesus in the air for His earthly saints and His coming to the earth with His saints. The first passage was spoken by our Lord Himself:

> *Watch ye therefore, and pray always, that ye may be accounted worthy to escape all these things that shall come to pass* [the Great Tribulation], *and to stand before the Son of man.*
> (Luke 21:36)

The second passage was written by Paul:

> *For the mystery of iniquity doth already work: only he who now letteth* [restrains] *will let* [restrain], *until he* [probably the church] *be taken out of the way. And then shall that Wicked* [the Antichrist] *be revealed, whom the Lord shall consume with the spirit of his mouth, and shall destroy with the brightness of his coming.*   (2 Thessalonians 2:7–8)

Remember, however, these two appearings do not constitute two comings, but two stages in one coming. Bearing in mind the distinction between these two stages in His second coming will help to solve many of the seeming discrepancies between different Bible texts on this subject.

The third stage is a succession of events that follow His coming to the earth. I will write on these at length in chapters four and five.

Openly and Publicly

Our Lord Jesus is coming again with great publicity. Our Lord Himself laid great emphasis on this fact and warned His disciples about all those false prophets and teachers who would proclaim a secret coming. He said,

> *Then if any man shall say unto you, Lo, here is Christ, or there; believe it not. For there shall arise false Christs, and false prophets, and shall show great signs and wonders; insomuch that, if it were possible, they shall deceive the very elect. Behold, I have told you before. Wherefore if they shall say unto you, Behold, he is in the desert; go not forth: behold, he is in the secret chambers; believe it not. For as the lightning cometh out of the east, and shineth even unto the west; so shall also the coming of the Son of man be.* (Matthew 24:23–27)

We are being told in these days that Jesus has come again in the form of some person or another, or in some new form of faith. One false teaching assures us that the second advent of the Lord Jesus Christ has already taken place. Another school of error would have us believe that the revelation of the doctrines of Christian Science to Mary Baker Eddy was the second coming of Christ. Another group of false disciples has gone to the heart of Iran to find our Lord. These "inner chamber" Christs and "obscure corner" Christs are impostors, long ago predicted and discredited.

If Christian people were more sensible and careful in their study of the Word on this subject, they would not so readily fall prey to these false teachings. Our Lord was careful to put us on our guards. We see in 1 Thessalonians 4:16 that His coming for His saints will be accompanied by a large amount of publicity: "*The Lord himself shall descend from heaven with a shout, with the voice of the archangel, and with the trump of God: and the dead in Christ shall rise first.*" The doctrine of the secret rapture of believers does not have scriptural support.

In the Clouds

When our Lord comes again, He will come in the clouds of heaven with power and glory. Regarding this He said,

> *And then shall appear the sign of the Son of man in heaven: and then shall all the tribes of the earth mourn, and they shall see the Son of man coming in the clouds of heaven with power and great glory.* (Matthew 24:30)

What did our Lord mean when He said He will come in the clouds? First of all, this is a literal description of the manner of His coming. But more than that, this sets forth the fact that He will come as a divine person and in divine glory. Everywhere in the Old Testament, Jehovah was the One who came in a cloud. In Exodus we read,

> *And the* Lord *said unto Moses, Lo, I come unto thee in a thick cloud, that the people may hear when I speak with thee, and believe thee for ever.* (Exodus 19:9)

Again, we read in Exodus 34:5, "*And the* Lord *descended in the cloud, and stood with him there, and proclaimed the name of the* Lord.*"

The psalmist sang,

> *The* Lord *reigneth; let the earth rejoice; let the multitude of isles be glad thereof. Clouds and darkness are round about him: righteousness and judgment are the habitation of his throne.* (Psalm 97:1–2)

Turning to the New Testament, we read,

> *While he yet spake, behold, a bright cloud overshadowed them: and behold a voice out of the cloud, which said, This is*

my beloved Son, in whom I am well pleased; hear ye him.
(Matthew 17:5)

In Psalm 104:3 it is written, "*Who layeth the beams of his chambers in the waters: who maketh the clouds his chariot: who walketh upon the wings of the wind,*" and in Isaiah 19:1, "*Behold, the* Lord *rideth upon a swift cloud.*"

From all these passages, it is plain that it is Jehovah who comes in the clouds or on a cloud. Therefore, to say that Jesus is coming in the clouds is to say that He is coming as a divine person in divine glory.

In the Father's Glory and with Angels

When our Lord Jesus comes again, He will come in the glory of His Father with the holy angels. He said so Himself. In one place, Matthew 16:27, He said, "*For the Son of man shall come in the glory of his Father with his angels; and then he shall reward every man according to his works.*" And in the book of Mark, He said,

Whosoever therefore shall be ashamed of me and of my words in this adulterous and sinful generation; of him also shall the Son of man be ashamed, when he cometh in the glory of his Father with the holy angels. (Mark 8:38)

In a similar strain, in 2 Thessalonians 1:7–8 the apostle Paul wrote that "*the Lord Jesus shall be revealed from heaven with his mighty angels, in flaming fire.*"

When Jesus came the first time, He came as a babe, wrapped in swaddling clothes and laid in a manger. He was despised and rejected of men; they did what they pleased with Him. The divine glory was hidden beneath the veil of flesh. But when He comes again, His divine glory and power will be revealed to every eye.

Even as He was manifested in His preexistent state in heaven to all the angelic world *"in the form of God"* (Philippians 2:6), so will He be manifested to us. While He will still be the Son of Man, He will be wearing the very form of God, clothed with the outwardly manifest glory of God.

Suddenly and Unexpectedly

The coming of our Lord Jesus will be sudden and unannounced. He will come unexpectedly and without warning. He said in Revelation 16:15, *"Behold, I come as a thief. Blessed is he that watcheth, and keepeth his garments, lest he walk naked, and they see his shame."* Some people believe that this verse refers to His coming to the believer at death, but the context and parallel passages show clearly that this is not the case. This verse refers to Christ's second coming.

The Holy Spirit, speaking through the apostle Paul, said to the believers in Thessalonica,

> For yourselves know perfectly that the day of the Lord so cometh as a thief in the night. For when they shall say, Peace and safety; then sudden destruction cometh upon them, as travail upon a woman with child; and they shall not escape.
> (1 Thessalonians 5:2–3)

When the Lord comes again, He will not find an expectant world, but an unexpectant world. The world will be engrossed in its usual occupations, as we see in the following passage:

> But as the days of Noe [Noah] were, so shall also the coming of the Son of man be. For as in the days that were before the flood they were eating and drinking, marrying and giving in marriage, until the day that Noe [Noah] entered into the ark,

and knew not until the flood came, and took them all away; so shall also the coming of the Son of man be.

(Matthew 24:37–39)

Men and women will not be gathered on hilltops in white robes waiting for the descent of their Lord. Everything will be going on just as usual. Then, without any announcement, without any previous warning, unexpectedly and suddenly, the trumpet of God will sound. *"The Lord himself shall descend from heaven with a shout, with the voice of the archangel, and with the trump of God"* (1 Thessalonians 4:16).

The attempt that so many are making to put together a complete and very definite chart of events leading up to our Lord's return loses sight of this clearly revealed fact about His coming. We may be sure that He is coming, but we cannot be sure of every detail regarding His coming. As the thief never sends word beforehand that He is coming, so our Lord will come without previous announcement. Our part is to be ready always, *"for in such an hour as ye think not the Son of man cometh"* (Matthew 24:44). We should always see to it that that day does not come upon us unexpectedly like a trap. How earnestly our Lord pleads with us,

And take heed to yourselves, lest at any time your hearts be overcharged with surfeiting [overindulgence], and drunkenness, and cares of this life, and so that day come upon you unawares. For as a snare shall it come on all them that dwell on the face of the whole earth. Watch ye therefore, and pray always, that ye may be accounted worthy to escape all these things that shall come to pass, and to stand before the Son of man. (Luke 21:34–36)

Chapter 4

A DAY OF JOY
AND SORROW

*Repent ye therefore, and be converted, that your sins may be
blotted out, when the times of refreshing shall come from the
presence of the Lord; and he shall send Jesus Christ, which before
was preached unto you: whom the heaven must receive until the
times of restitution of all things, which God hath spoken by the
mouth of all his holy prophets since the world began.*
—Acts 3:19–21

We come now to the brightest, gladdest part of this whole subject: the results of our Lord's return to this earth. These results are
revealed in His Word. They are such that the very contemplation
of them will fill the believer's heart not only with hope and longing,
but with gladness and ecstasy.

These results are manifold. They may be classified under seven
headings: first, the results regarding God; second, the results
regarding the church and individual believers; third, the results
regarding Israel; fourth, the results regarding the nations; fifth,
the results regarding human society as a whole; sixth, the results
regarding the Antichrist and the Devil; and seventh, the results
regarding the physical universe.

I will discuss the first three categories in this chapter, saving
the other four categories for the next chapter.

Results Regarding God

The return of our Lord will result in new glory to God. We read in Isaiah 40:5, "*The glory of the LORD shall be revealed, and all flesh shall see it together.*" The context clearly shows that it is at the coming of the Lord that this prophecy is to be fulfilled. (See verses 3, 9, and 10.)

The glory of God has already been revealed in creation. (See Psalm 19:1.) It is being revealed from century to century in history, and it was revealed in the person and work of Jesus Christ at His first coming. But the full revelation of the glory of God will be in connection with Christ's second coming. That is the first reason that we should desire it, so that there may be new glory given to the name of Him whom we love and worship.

When our Lord returns, He Himself will reign as King. We are told this repeatedly in the New Testament, as well as in the Old. In the parable of the ten pounds, our Lord compared Himself to "*a certain nobleman [who] went into a far country to receive for himself a kingdom, and to return*" (Luke 19:12). In the fifteenth verse He said, "*He...returned, having received the kingdom.*" Again, Jesus said in Matthew 25:31, "*When the Son of man shall come in his glory, and all the holy angels with him, then shall he sit upon the throne of his glory.*"

We find this representation of our Lord Jesus reigning as King over and over again in the Old Testament also. For example, in the book of Jeremiah we read,

> *Behold, the days come, saith the LORD, that I will raise unto David a righteous Branch, and a King shall reign and prosper, and shall execute judgment and justice in the earth. In his days Judah shall be saved, and Israel shall dwell safely: and this is his name whereby he shall be called, THE LORD OUR RIGHTEOUSNESS.* (Jeremiah 23:5–6)

Referring to the same period, Jehovah declared in Psalm 2:6, "*Yet have I set my king upon my holy hill of Zion.*" Through the prophet Zechariah, the Spirit of God set forth the same truth in a way that emphasizes the deity of our Lord: "*And the* LORD *shall be king over all the earth: in that day shall there be one* LORD, *and his name one*" (Zechariah 14:9).

The last book of the Bible returns to this reign of Christ again and again. For example, we read,

And I saw heaven opened, and behold a white horse; and he that sat upon him was called Faithful and True, and in righteousness he doth judge and make war. His eyes were as a flame of fire, and on his head were many crowns; and he had a name written, that no man knew, but he himself. And he was clothed with a vesture [garment] dipped in blood: and his name is called The Word of God. And the armies which were in heaven followed him upon white horses, clothed in fine linen, white and clean. And out of his mouth goeth a sharp sword, that with it he should smite the nations: and he shall rule them with a rod of iron: and he treadeth the winepress of the fierceness and wrath of Almighty God. And he hath on his vesture [garment] and on his thigh a name written, KING OF KINGS, AND LORD OF LORDS.   (Revelation 19:11–16)

And again it is written in the book of Revelation,

And I saw thrones, and they sat upon them, and judgment was given unto them: and I saw the souls of them that were beheaded for the witness of Jesus, and for the word of God, and which had not worshipped the beast, neither his image, neither had received his mark upon their foreheads, or in their hands; and they lived and reigned with Christ a thousand years.   (Revelation 20:4)

Yes, it is clearly revealed in the Word of God that the time is coming when our Lord Jesus, who was once *"despised and rejected of men"* (Isaiah 53:3), will be acknowledged as King and will rule here on the earth. The time is fast approaching when the angel will sound his trumpet and there will be great voices in heaven saying, *"The kingdoms of this world are become the kingdoms of our Lord, and of his Christ; and he shall reign for ever and ever"* (Revelation 11:15). Later in this chapter and in the next chapter, we will consider the characteristics and the results of this blessed reign of our Lord.

Results Regarding the Church and Individual Believers

Next we will examine the effects that our Lord's return will have on the church and on individual believers.

The Dead in Christ Raised

The first result of our Lord's return that applies to believers is that, immediately upon His coming in the air, those who have died in Christ will rise.

> *For this we say unto you by the word of the Lord, that we which are alive and remain unto the coming of the Lord shall not prevent [precede] them which are asleep. For the Lord himself shall descend from heaven with a shout, with the voice of the archangel, and with the trump of God: and the dead in Christ shall rise first.*   (1 Thessalonians 4:15–16)

Until our Lord comes, the bodies of believers who have passed out of this world before that great event *"sleep in the dust of the earth"* (Daniel 12:2). Their spirits are unclothed (see 2 Corinthians 5:4); their spirits are *"absent from the body"* and *"present with the Lord"* (2 Corinthians 5:8). However, immediately upon the sounding of the trumpet of God and the accompanying descent of our Lord, these bodies that sleep in the dust of the earth will be raised; the spirits of believers will no longer be unclothed, but *"clothed upon with our house which is from heaven"* (2 Corinthians 5:2).

The Bodies of Living Believers Transformed

Immediately following the resurrection of the dead in Christ, the bodies of living believers will be changed from their present state of humiliation into the likeness of His glorious body. The bodies that we now have are not the bodies that we will have. As we saw earlier,

> We look for the Saviour, the Lord Jesus Christ: who shall change our vile body, that it may be fashioned like unto his glorious body, according to the working whereby he is able even to subdue all things unto himself.   (Philippians 3:20–21)

It is then, and only then, that we will be fully manifested outwardly as children of God.

We cannot help but feel the limitations of our present bodies, as good as they are for many purposes, and we often *"groan within ourselves, waiting for the adoption, to wit, the redemption of our body"* (Romans 8:23). The redemption of our bodies will come when He comes; then the work of redemption will be completed. We will each have a body like His own glorious body. This body will be incorruptible, imperishable, glorious, and powerful. (See 1 Corinthians 15:42–43.) Our days of weariness and weakness will be forever ended; our bodies will be able to accomplish all that our spirits purpose. They will be free from all the limitations of earth and will be clothed upon with all the glory and power that pertains to the heavenly world. In a word, they will be heavenly bodies. (See Corinthians 15:47–49.) Furthermore, we will no longer be subject to death, but will be like the angels. (See Luke 20:35–36.)

Our very bodies will be luminous, shining, dazzling, bright like the sun. This is not imagination and poetry, but revealed fact. Our Lord said in Matthew 13:43, *"Then shall the righteous shine forth as the sun in the kingdom of their Father."* This is not a part of the figurative language of the parable He was telling in this chapter (the parable of the wheat and the tares), but a part of the literal language of the interpretation of the parable. In a similar way, centuries before Christ, it had been revealed by Jehovah to Daniel that *"they that be wise shall shine as the brightness of the firmament; and they that turn many to righteousness as the stars for ever and ever"* (Daniel 12:3). When Jesus was being glorified on the Mount of Transfiguration in front of His disciples, His face shone as the sun, and His garments became as *"white as the light"* (Matthew 17:2). Our bodies will be like His!

This resurrection body will be the consummation of our adoption, our placing as sons. Through our resurrection bodies, it will be outwardly obvious that we are sons of God. Before His incarnation, Christ was *"in the form of God"* (Philippians 2:6), that is, in the visible appearance of God, and we will also be in this form when we receive our resurrection bodies at His return.

The Meeting in the Air

The dead in Christ having been raised and the bodies of living believers having been transformed, they will all be caught up together to meet the Lord in the air, and so we will always *"be with the Lord"* (1 Thessalonians 4:17). It is especially to receive us unto Himself that Jesus Christ will come again at all. This He declared to His disciples on the night before He left them. He said, *"If I go and prepare a place for you, I will come again, and receive you unto myself; that where I am, there ye may be also"* (John 14:3).

It is primarily love for His own that will draw our Lord Jesus back to this earth again. He loves us so much that He does not want to be apart from us. He will send no mere messenger for us; He will come Himself. *"I will come again"* are His thrilling words. And it is to receive us unto Himself that He will come—not merely to receive us into heaven, but unto Himself.

His words indicate His intense longing for us. How He longs to gather us unto Himself and embrace us! We long for Him during His absence from us, but not as He longs for us. Even heaven itself is a lonely place to Him without us. Earth ought to be a lonely place to us without Him.

One commentator's remarks on His words are worth quoting. Speaking of the believer and Christ's attitude toward him, he said, "He presses him to His heart, so to speak, while bearing him away. There is an infinite tenderness in these last words, *'unto myself.'* It is for Himself that He seems to rejoice and look to this moment, which will be the end of all separation."

Made like Him

At the return of our Lord Jesus and as a result of our then beholding Him as He is, we will be made like Him. One of the most marvelous promises in the whole Bible was uttered by John, the beloved disciple. He said,

> *Beloved, now are we the sons of God, and it doth not yet appear what we shall be: but we know that, when he shall appear, we shall be like him; for we shall see him as he is.*
>
> (1 John 3:2)

The perfect beholding of our Lord in that day will transform us into the perfect image of Him. Even in this life, it is through beholding the glory of the Lord that we are *"changed into the same image from glory to glory"* (2 Corinthians 3:18); that is, each new view of Him imparts something more of His glory to us. But now we only see in a mirror dimly. (See 1 Corinthians 13:12.)

Consequently, our reflection of His glory is imperfect. Then, we will see Him face to face in His undimmed glory and will perfectly reflect it. When we are transformed into His perfect likeness, spiritually as well as bodily, our Lord will be *"glorified in his saints"* (2 Thessalonians 1:10), not merely glorified by us, but also in us. His glory will be fully revealed in what we are in that day. Not only will He appear in all the fullness of His glory, but we also will *"appear with him in glory"* (Colossians 3:4).

I have often labored to uplift the one who has fallen deeply into sin, the one whose character has been so disfigured by the wicked life he has led that the process of salvation has been hindered by many a discouraging fall. Oftentimes, I have felt tempted to give up the battle for his redemption. But I have taken new courage as I have thought of 1 John 3:2. I have said to myself, "Although this person I am trying to help seems so little like the Lord that it seems like a waste of time to do anything more to help him, still, someday, when our Lord comes and he gets one glimpse of Him as He is, this person will be so transformed into His perfect image that he will be just like Him."

Sometimes, too, when I am discouraged over my own failures and almost overwhelmed with the thought of how unlike I am to my Master, the glad thought has thrilled me that it will not always be so. Someday, that glad day when the Lord Himself descends from heaven with a shout, with the voice of the archangel, and with the trumpet of God; when I am caught up to meet Him; and when I see Him as He is, I, too, will be just like Him, in all the infinite perfection of His character. Then, I will attain *"unto the measure of the stature of the fulness of Christ"* (Ephesians 4:13).

Married to Christ

Now, a still more wonderful result will follow: our Lord Jesus will be united in marriage with the church, and the marriage supper of the Lamb will be celebrated. John said,

And I heard as it were the voice of a great multitude, and as the voice of many waters, and as the voice of mighty thunderings, saying, Alleluia: for the Lord God omnipotent reigneth. Let us be glad and rejoice, and give honour to him: for the marriage of the Lamb is come, and his wife hath made herself ready. And to her was granted that she should be arrayed in fine linen, clean and white: for the fine linen is the righteousness of saints. And he saith unto me, Write, Blessed are they which are called unto the marriage supper of the Lamb.

(Revelation 19:6–9)

These words are so remarkable that it is no wonder that the angel who spoke them to John felt the necessity of adding, *"These are the true sayings of God"* (verse 9). It is impossible for us to fathom now all the depth of meaning that there is in this passage, and this is a place where speculation should be very guarded. However, this much has been revealed: in the relationship between Christ and His church, and there alone, the full significance of marriage has been realized. (See Ephesians 5:31–32.) This intimate relationship between Christ and His church will be fully experienced at His coming again.

Servants Receive Rewards

At the return of our Lord, each one of His servants will receive his reward: *"For the Son of man shall come in the glory of his Father with his angels; and then he shall reward every man according to his works"* (Matthew 16:27). It is not at death, but at the coming of the Lord, that we receive our full reward.

All those who anticipate His return with delight will receive a crown of righteousness. It was in anticipation of this that Paul, as he sat in his prison cell in Rome awaiting execution, wrote,

I have fought a good fight, I have finished my course, I have kept the faith: henceforth there is laid up for me a crown of

righteousness, which the Lord, the righteous judge, shall give me at that day: and not to me only, but unto all them also that love his appearing.   (2 Timothy 4:7–8)

The faithful shepherds of the flock will receive a crown of glory that does not fade away. It was with this in view that the apostle Peter exhorted the elders to care for the church:

Feed the flock of God which is among you, taking the oversight thereof, not by constraint, but willingly; not for filthy lucre [dishonest gain], but of a ready mind; neither as being lords over God's heritage, but being ensamples [examples] to the flock. And when the chief Shepherd shall appear, ye shall receive a crown of glory that fadeth not away.   (1 Peter 5:2–4)

Saints Reign with Christ

When our Lord returns, His people will live and reign with Him. John said,

And I saw thrones, and they sat upon them, and judgment was given unto them: and I saw the souls of them that were beheaded for the witness of Jesus, and for the word of God, and which had not worshipped the beast, neither his image, neither had received his mark upon their foreheads, or in their hands; and they lived and reigned with Christ a thousand years.   (Revelation 20:4)

This passage seems to refer primarily to the tribulation saints, but by implication it includes all those who have believed in Jesus in this present dispensation. Certainly the bride must reign with her Husband. Indeed, we are explicitly told in Revelation 5:9–10 that our Lord has made those whom He purchased from every tribe, tongue, people, and nation, to be a kingdom and to be priests unto God, and they *"shall reign on the earth"* (verse 10).

Results Regarding Israel

Next I would like to discuss the effects that our Lord's return will have on Israel. As you will see, these effects are many.

Joy and Sorrow

There will be great joy among God's people Israel because of our Lord's return. The prophet Isaiah, speaking of that day, said,

> *And it shall be said in that day, Lo, this is our God; we have waited for him, and he will save us: this is the LORD; we have waited for him, we will be glad and rejoice in his salvation.*
> (Isaiah 25:9)

This can hardly be limited to Israel, but the context seems clearly to imply that the primary reference is to them. Why Israel will rejoice will become evident enough as we study the further results of His coming again.

But as great as their joy will be, it will begin with a great mourning—mourning over their sin, and especially over their former rejection of their King. The prophet Zechariah told us,

> *In that day shall the LORD defend the inhabitants of Jerusalem; and he that is feeble among them at that day shall be as David; and the house of David shall be as God, as the angel of the LORD before them. And it shall come to pass in that day, that I will seek to destroy all the nations that come against Jerusalem. And I will pour upon the house of David, and upon the inhabitants of Jerusalem, the spirit of grace and of supplications: and they shall look upon me whom they have pierced, and they shall mourn for him, as one mourneth for his only son, and shall be in bitterness for him, as one that is in bitterness for his firstborn. In that day shall there be a great*

mourning in Jerusalem, as the mourning of Hadadrimmon in the valley of Megiddon. And the land shall mourn, every family apart; the family of the house of David apart, and their wives apart; the family of the house of Nathan apart, and their wives apart; the family of the house of Levi apart, and their wives apart; the family of Shimei apart, and their wives apart; all the families that remain, every family apart, and their wives apart. (Zechariah 12:8–14)

But following their mourning, *"a fountain"* will be opened *"for sin and for uncleanness"* (Zechariah 13:1), and Jehovah Himself will go forth to fight against all their enemies. (See Zechariah 14:1–3.)

Deliverance in the Day of Crisis

The return of our Lord Jesus will result in the deliverance of the people of Israel in the day when their trials and sufferings will culminate. We read further in Zechariah,

Behold, the day of the Lord *cometh, and thy spoil shall be divided in the midst of thee. For I will gather all nations against Jerusalem to battle; and the city shall be taken, and the houses rifled, and the women ravished; and half of the city shall go forth into captivity, and the residue of the people shall not be cut off from the city. Then shall the* Lord *go forth, and fight against those nations, as when he fought in the day of battle. And his feet shall stand in that day upon the mount of Olives, which is before Jerusalem on the east, and the mount of Olives shall cleave in the midst thereof toward the east and toward the west, and there shall be a very great valley; and half of the mountain shall remove toward the north, and half of it toward the south.* (Zechariah 14:1–4)

Present-day events seem to indicate that we are fast approaching the day when these promises will be fulfilled.

A Return to Their Land

In connection with the return of our Lord, the children of Israel will be gathered together from among the nations, from the four corners of the earth, and brought again into their own land. This is promised over and over again in the prophecies of the Old Testament. We read in Isaiah,

> And it shall come to pass in that day, that the Lord shall set his hand again the second time to recover the remnant of his people, which shall be left, from Assyria, and from Egypt, and from Pathros, and from Cush, and from Elam, and from Shinar, and from Hamath, and from the islands of the sea. And he shall set up an ensign for the nations, and shall assemble the outcasts of Israel, and gather together the dispersed of Judah from the four corners of the earth.   (Isaiah 11:11–12)

Similarly, we read in Ezekiel 36:24, "For I will take you from among the heathen, and gather you out of all countries, and will bring you into your own land." And another verse in Ezekiel says,

> Thus saith the Lord GOD; Behold, I will take the children of Israel from among the heathen, whither they be gone, and will gather them on every side, and bring them into their own land.   (Ezekiel 37:21)

And in the prophecy of Zephaniah we also read,

> Behold, at that time I will undo all that afflict thee: and I will save her that halteth, and gather her that was driven out; and I will get them praise and fame in every land where they have been put to shame. At that time will I bring you again, even in the time that I gather you: for I will make you a name and a praise among all people of the earth, when I turn back your captivity before your eyes, saith the LORD.
>   (Zephaniah 3:19–20)

All of these prophecies will be fulfilled to the very letter in connection with the second coming of Christ.

Ephraim and Judah United

At the time of our Lord's return, Ephraim and Judah, who have been so long divided from one another, will be united in one nation under one King, David. This is made very plain in the book of Ezekiel:

> *Say unto them, Thus saith the Lord GOD; Behold, I will take the stick of Joseph, which is in the hand of Ephraim, and the tribes of Israel his fellows, and will put them with him, even with the stick of Judah, and make them one stick, and they shall be one in mine hand....And I will make them one nation in the land upon the mountains of Israel; and one king shall be king to them all: and they shall be no more two nations, neither shall they be divided into two kingdoms any more at all....And David my servant shall be king over them; and they all shall have one shepherd: they shall also walk in my judgments, and observe my statutes, and do them.*
>
> (Ezekiel 37:19, 22, 24)

Safety and Salvation

Closely connected with what has just been said, it is revealed in God's Word that because of our Lord's return, Judah will be saved and Israel will dwell safely.

> *Behold, the days come, saith the LORD, that I will raise unto David a righteous Branch, and a King shall reign and prosper, and shall execute judgment and justice in the earth. In his days Judah shall be saved, and Israel shall dwell safely.*
>
> (Jeremiah 23:5–6)

There will be a national salvation of all Israelites then upon the earth. As Paul put it,

> And so all Israel shall be saved: as it is written, There shall come out of Sion the Deliverer, and shall turn away ungodliness from Jacob: for this is my covenant unto them, when I shall take away their sins. (Romans 11:26–27)

"*The gifts and calling of God are without repentance*" (Romans 11:29). Although the people of Israel have proven untrue to the covenant of God, God remains faithful. At present they are enemies of the Gospel for our sake, but concerning the election they are beloved for the fathers' sake; and in due time, in connection with the return of our Lord, God will have mercy on them all. (See verses 28–32.) The people of Israel will be cleansed from all their filthiness and from all their idols. New hearts will be given unto them, and new spirits put within them. Stony hearts will be taken away from them, and they will be given hearts of flesh. God will put His Spirit within them and cause them to walk in His statutes, and they will keep His judgments and do them. This in every detail is a matter of divine prediction. Jehovah Himself said through the prophet Ezekiel,

> Neither shall they defile themselves any more with their idols, nor with their detestable things, nor with any of their transgressions: but I will save them out of all their dwellingplaces, wherein they have sinned, and will cleanse them: so shall they be my people, and I will be their God. (Ezekiel 37:23)

In the preceding chapter of Ezekiel, He had already said,

> Then will I sprinkle clean water upon you, and ye shall be clean: from all your filthiness, and from all your idols, will I cleanse you. A new heart also will I give you, and a new spirit will I put within you: and I will take away the stony heart out

*of your flesh, and I will give you an heart of flesh. And I will
put my spirit within you, and cause you to walk in my statutes,
and ye shall keep my judgments, and do them....I will also
save you from all your uncleannesses: and I will call for the
corn, and will increase it, and lay no famine upon you.*

(Ezekiel 36:25–27, 29)

The same thought was expressed in other words through the
prophet Jeremiah. We read,

Behold, the days come, saith the LORD, *that I will make a new
covenant with the house of Israel, and with the house of Judah:
not according to the covenant that I made with their fathers in
the day that I took them by the hand to bring them out of the
land of Egypt; which my covenant they brake, although I was
an husband unto them, saith the* LORD: *but this shall be the
covenant that I will make with the house of Israel; After those
days, saith the* LORD, *I will put my law in their inward parts,
and write it in their hearts; and will be their God, and they
shall be my people. And they shall teach no more every man
his neighbour, and every man his brother, saying, Know the*
LORD: *for they shall all know me, from the least of them unto
the greatest of them, saith the* LORD: *for I will forgive their
iniquity, and I will remember their sin no more.*

(Jeremiah 31:31–34)

A Golden Age

Because of the return of our Lord Jesus and the events that
grow out of that return, Israel will be wondrously multiplied. The
wasted, desolate, and ruined cities will be rebuilt, and the desolate
land will become like the Garden of Eden. Jerusalem will be called
"a city of truth" (Zechariah 8:3) and will be filled with peace, pros-
perity, and gladness. The books of the Old Testament prophets

abound with predictions of this golden age that is coming to Israel. In Ezekiel we read,

> *Thus saith the Lord GOD; I will yet for this be inquired of by the house of Israel, to do it for them; I will increase them with men like a flock. As the holy flock, as the flock of Jerusalem in her solemn feasts; so shall the waste cities be filled with flocks of men: and they shall know that I am the LORD.*
>
> (Ezekiel 36:37–38)

And in Jeremiah 31:27 we read, "*Behold, the days come, saith the LORD, that I will sow the house of Israel and the house of Judah with the seed of man, and with the seed of beast.*" Turning again to Ezekiel, we read,

> *Thus saith the Lord GOD; In the day that I shall have cleansed you from all your iniquities I will also cause you to dwell in the cities, and the wastes shall be builded. And the desolate land shall be tilled, whereas it lay desolate in the sight of all that passed by. And they shall say, This land that was desolate is become like the garden of Eden; and the waste and desolate and ruined cities are become fenced, and are inhabited. Then the heathen that are left round about you shall know that I the LORD build the ruined places, and plant that that was desolate: I the LORD have spoken it, and I will do it.*
>
> (Ezekiel 36:33–36)

Zechariah also painted his picture of the glad coming days when judgment will be followed by blessing. We read,

> *Thus saith the LORD; I am returned unto Zion, and will dwell in the midst of Jerusalem: and Jerusalem shall be called a city of truth; and the mountain of the LORD of hosts the holy mountain. Thus saith the LORD of hosts; There shall yet old men and old women dwell in the streets of Jerusalem, and every man with his staff in his hand for very age. And the*

streets of the city shall be full of boys and girls playing in the
streets thereof.   (Zechariah 8:3–5)

This is not, as it is so often taken to be, a picture of heaven; it is a picture of the literal Jerusalem in the glad day that is coming as a result of our Lord's return to this earth. Israel in that day will be greatly exalted above the nations. We read in the same chapter of Zechariah,

Thus saith the LORD of hosts; In those days it shall come to
pass, that ten men shall take hold out of all languages of the
nations, even shall take hold of the skirt of him that is a Jew,
saying, We will go with you: for we have heard that God is
with you.   (Zechariah 8:23)

This same thought is more fully expressed in the book of Isaiah:

Thus saith the Lord GOD, Behold, I will lift up mine hand to
the Gentiles, and set up my standard to the people: and they
shall bring thy sons in their arms, and thy daughters shall be
carried upon their shoulders. And kings shall be thy nursing
fathers, and their queens thy nursing mothers: they shall bow
down to thee with their face toward the earth, and lick up the
dust of thy feet; and thou shalt know that I am the LORD: for
they shall not be ashamed that wait for me.

                              (Isaiah 49:22–23)

It is very plain to anyone who carefully reads this chapter in Isaiah and notes exactly what is said that this cannot refer to the restoration of the church, as some have interpreted it, but to the future glory of Israel, God's earthly people.

The World's Greatest Missionaries

Having been restored and exalted above the nations, Israel will go forth as preachers of the glory of Jehovah to all nations.

In the last chapter of Isaiah's prophecy, Jehovah said,

And I will set a sign among them, and I will send those that escape of them unto the nations, to Tarshish, Pul, and Lud, that draw the bow, to Tubal, and Javan, to the isles afar off, that have not heard my fame, neither have seen my glory; and they shall declare my glory among the Gentiles.

(Isaiah 66:19)

Although the vast majority of Israelites today are rejecting the Lord Jesus, they are still destined to become the greatest missionaries in the world's history. Paul, a Jew who had once bitterly opposed the Lord, did mighty things as the Apostle to the Gentiles after his conversion. This gives us a hint of what the whole Jewish nation will do when they have been converted and go forth as missionaries in that great coming era.

Chapter 5

PEACE AND PUNISHMENT

*He shall have dominion also from sea to sea, and from
the river unto the ends of the earth. They that dwell in the
wilderness shall bow before him; and his enemies shall lick
the dust. The kings of Tarshish and of the isles shall bring
presents: the kings of Sheba and Seba shall offer gifts. Yea, all
kings shall fall down before him: all nations shall serve him.*
—Psalm 72:8–11

Picking up where we left off in the last chapter, we will examine
the results of our Lord's return on the nations and the unsaved, on
human society, on the Antichrist and the Devil, and on the physical
universe.

Results Regarding the Nations and the Unsaved

I would like to turn our attention to the effects of our Lord's
return on the nations and on unregenerate individuals. When I
speak of nations, I am referring to all the peoples of the earth except
the nation of Israel, which we just covered in the previous chapter.

Universal Mourning

The first result of our Lord's return regarding the nations will
be a universal mourning over Him. We read in Revelation 1:7,

"Behold, he cometh with clouds; and every eye shall see him, and they also which pierced him: and all kindreds of the earth shall wail because of him." Our Lord Jesus Himself declared the same fact. He said to His disciples, in expounding to them the facts concerning His own coming,

> And then shall appear the sign of the Son of man in heaven: and then shall all the tribes of the earth mourn, and they shall see the Son of man coming in the clouds of heaven with power and great glory.   (Matthew 24:30)

The gladdest day of all for His people will be the saddest day of all for those who are not His people. For His people it will be the consummation of all their hopes and dreams, but for those who have rejected Him, it will be the shattering of all their hopes and dreams.

Universal Judgment

All the nations will be gathered before Him for judgment. He will separate the people one from another as the shepherd divides his sheep from his goats. The Lord Jesus said the following about this:

> When the Son of man shall come in his glory, and all the holy angels with him, then shall he sit upon the throne of his glory: and before him shall be gathered all nations: and he shall separate them one from another, as a shepherd divideth his sheep from the goats.   (Matthew 25:31–32)

Then will follow the judgment of those nations then living on the earth: the sheep on His right hand will go away into eternal life, and the goats on His left hand into eternal punishment. This is plainly shown in the same chapter of Matthew:

> Then shall the King say unto them on his right hand, Come, ye blessed of my Father, inherit the kingdom prepared for you from

the foundation of the world: for I was an hungered, and ye gave me meat: I was thirsty, and ye gave me drink: I was a stranger, and ye took me in: naked, and ye clothed me: I was sick, and ye visited me: I was in prison, and ye came unto me. Then shall the righteous answer him, saying, Lord, when saw we thee an hungered, and fed thee? or thirsty, and gave thee drink? When saw we thee a stranger, and took thee in? or naked, and clothed thee? Or when saw we thee sick, or in prison, and came unto thee? And the King shall answer and say unto them, Verily I say unto you, Inasmuch as ye have done it unto one of the least of these my brethren, ye have done it unto me. Then shall he say also unto them on the left hand, Depart from me, ye cursed, into everlasting fire, prepared for the devil and his angels: for I was an hungered, and ye gave me no meat: I was thirsty, and ye gave me no drink: I was a stranger, and ye took me not in: naked, and ye clothed me not: sick, and in prison, and ye visited me not. Then shall they also answer him, saying, Lord, when saw we thee an hungered, or athirst, or a stranger, or naked, or sick, or in prison, and did not minister unto thee? Then shall he answer them, saying, Verily I say unto you, Inasmuch as ye did it not to one of the least of these, ye did it not to me. And these shall go away into everlasting punishment: but the righteous into life eternal. (Matthew 25:34–46)

A Widespread Turning to the Lord

At the return of our Lord Jesus, all the Gentiles who are called by His name will seek after the Lord, as we see in the book of Acts:

After this I will return, and will build again the tabernacle of David, which is fallen down; and I will build again the ruins thereof, and I will set it up: that the residue of men might seek after the Lord, and all the Gentiles, upon whom my name is called. (Acts 15:16–17)

We also see this in the book of Zechariah: *"Yea, many people and strong nations shall come to seek the Lord of hosts in Jerusalem, and to pray before the Lord"* (Zechariah 8:22). There will be a great turning unto the Lord, as we see again in the book of Isaiah:

> And it shall come to pass in the last days, that the mountain of the Lord's house shall be established in the top of the mountains, and shall be exalted above the hills; and all nations shall flow unto it. And many people shall go and say, Come ye, and let us go up to the mountain of the Lord, to the house of the God of Jacob; and he will teach us of his ways, and we will walk in his paths: for out of Zion shall go forth the law, and the word of the Lord from Jerusalem.   (Isaiah 2:2–3)

The question naturally arises here, How can this be if immediately upon His coming, the nations are gathered before Him, judged, separated, and assigned to their eternal destinies? The answer is very simple. Nowhere does the Bible say that immediately upon His coming the nations will be gathered, judged, separated, and assigned to their eternal destinies. Our difficulty here, as in many other places, arises from the fact that we assume what the Bible never asserts or implies, that is, that these things are all crowded into a day or a few days or even a year.

All these events are connected with and result from His coming, but they probably take time to develop. Prophecies were never intended to give us the details and the order of all the events connected with the Lord's coming. It is never the method of prophecy to give all the details and the exact order of events. The great important facts necessary to keep us watching and to cheer our hearts and to fire us for our work are given in outline form. But we should always bear in mind that while prophecy is exactly and literally true in every word, and will be exactly and literally fulfilled, nevertheless, prophecy is not a detailed list of sequential events.

The Ungodly Are Punished

As a result of the return of our Lord Jesus, and as a result of His glorious reign that follows His return, all who are rebellious against Him will be shattered. *"Thou* [Christ] *shalt break them,"* said the Holy Spirit through the psalmist, *"with a rod of iron; thou shalt dash them in pieces like a potter's vessel"* (Psalm 2:9). Our Lord will

> *Execute judgment upon all, and* [will] *convince all that are ungodly among them of all their ungodly deeds which they have ungodly committed, and of all their hard speeches which ungodly sinners have spoken against him.*   (Jude 1:15)

He will *"punish the inhabitants of the earth for their iniquity"* (Isaiah 26:21). Second Thessalonians describes the punishment that Christ will mete out:

> *In flaming fire taking vengeance on them that know not God, and that obey not the gospel of our Lord Jesus Christ: who shall be punished with everlasting destruction from the presence of the Lord, and from the glory of his power.*
> (2 Thessalonians 1:8–9)

We can learn what *"destruction"* means in this passage from a comparison of Revelation 17:11 with Revelation 19:20 and Revelation 20:10. In Revelation 17:11 we are told that the Beast *"goeth into perdition."* The word here translated *"perdition"* is the same Greek word that is elsewhere translated *"destruction"* and might well have been so translated here to help us avoid confusion. If we can find out where the Beast goes, we will then know what *"perdition,"* or *"destruction,"* means. In Revelation 19:20 we have a very explicit statement of where the Beast goes. Here we are told,

> *The beast was taken, and with him the false prophet that wrought miracles before him, with which he deceived them*

that had received the mark of the beast, and them that wor-
shipped his image. These both were cast alive into a lake of fire
burning with brimstone.   (Revelation 19:20)

But what becomes of the Beast in that lake of fire? Is he annihi-
lated? Does he lose conscious existence? This question is answered
in the next chapter: *"And the devil that deceived them was cast into the*
lake of fire and brimstone, where the beast and the false prophet are"
(Revelation 20:10). Let us remember that this is after a thousand
years, and we see that the Beast and the False Prophet are still there.
They have not ceased to exist in the thousand years that have elapsed
since they were put there, and we are furthermore told in the remain-
der of the verse that they *"shall be tormented day and night for ever and*
ever." The words translated *"shall be tormented"* in this passage can
only refer to conscious torment. Therefore, God's own definition of
"destruction" is *"a condition of conscious and awful torment."*

All Remaining People Serve Jesus

However, there is a bright side to the results of our Lord's
coming even in regard to the nations. It is clearly taught that every-
one who is left of the nations and kings and princes will worship
and serve Jesus Christ. We read in Zechariah,

And it shall come to pass, that every one that is left of all the
nations which came against Jerusalem shall even go up from
year to year to worship the King, the LORD of hosts, and to
keep the feast of tabernacles.   (Zechariah 14:16)

And in Isaiah we read,

Thus saith the LORD, the Redeemer of Israel, and his Holy
One, to him whom man despiseth, to him whom the nation
abhorreth, to a servant of rulers [to Jesus Christ], *Kings shall*
see and arise, princes also shall worship, because of the LORD

that is faithful, and the Holy One of Israel, and he shall choose
thee.   (Isaiah 49:7)

Isaiah was referring to the kings and princes of the Gentiles. This is evident from the verse that immediately precedes: "*I will also give thee for a light to the Gentiles, that thou mayest be my salvation unto the end of the earth.*"

Along the same lines, in Revelation 15:4 we read, "*Who shall not fear thee, O Lord, and glorify thy name? for thou only art holy: for all nations shall come and worship before thee.*" And in the wonderful prophecy concerning our Lord found in the book of Psalms, we read, "*Ask of me, and I shall give thee the heathen for thine inheritance, and the uttermost parts of the earth for thy possession*" (Psalm 2:8). And in another marvelous prophetic picture of the Lord Jesus in the book of Psalms, we read,

He shall have dominion also from sea to sea, and from the river
unto the ends of the earth. They that dwell in the wilderness
shall bow before him; and his enemies shall lick the dust. The
kings of Tarshish and of the isles shall bring presents: the kings
of Sheba and Seba shall offer gifts. Yea, all kings shall fall down
before him: all nations shall serve him.   (Psalm 72:8–11)

Similarly, Zechariah told us, "*He shall speak peace unto the heathen: and his dominion shall be from sea even to sea, and from the river even to the ends of the earth*" (Zechariah 9:10). To sum it all up, "*the kingdoms of this world [will] become the kingdoms of our Lord, and of his Christ; and he shall reign for ever and ever*" (Revelation 11:15.)

Results Regarding Human Society

The return of our Lord Jesus will affect human society as a whole.

A Time of Peace and Plenty

At the return of our Lord Jesus and as a result of that return, war will cease, peace and plenty will reign, and the righteous will flourish. This is declared over and over again in the prophetic Scriptures. For example, we read in Isaiah,

> *And it shall come to pass in the last days, that the mountain of the Lord's house shall be established in the top of the mountains, and shall be exalted above the hills; and all nations shall flow unto it.....And he shall judge among the nations, and shall rebuke many people: and they shall beat their swords into plowshares, and their spears into pruninghooks: nation shall not lift up sword against nation, neither shall they learn war any more.* (Isaiah 2:2, 4)

We find a similar picture of these glad coming days in the prophecy of Micah:

> *And he shall judge among many people, and rebuke strong nations afar off; and they shall beat their swords into plowshares, and their spears into pruninghooks: nation shall not lift up a sword against nation, neither shall they learn war any more. But they shall sit every man under his vine and under his fig tree; and none shall make them afraid: for the mouth of the LORD of hosts hath spoken it.* (Micah 4:3–4)

Then and only then will we enjoy what the greatest statesmen of the present day are trying to accomplish. We now have our peace conferences, and they have accomplished something, but they will prove utterly futile to accomplish all that is in the minds and hearts of our greatest statesmen. While we talk peace, we are increasing our navies and our armies. We are squandering untold millions on schemes for destroying the lives of our fellow men and for the protection and extension of our own nation. We talk of disarmament, but we all know it is not coming. All our present peace plans will end in the most awful wars and conflicts this world has ever seen.

Nevertheless, there is a good day coming when war will be at an end, when there will be universal peace, when there will no longer be conflict between nation and nation, or between class and class. There will be no more strikes, because strikes will not be needed. Industrial wars, as well as wars between nations, will be over, and peace and plenty will reign. The prophetic vision of the psalmist will be realized: *"In his days shall the righteous flourish; and abundance of peace so long as the moon endureth"* (Psalm 72:7). All this is to be realized at, and as a result of, the return of our Lord Jesus.

The Earth Is Filled with the Knowledge of the Lord

The whole earth will be full of the knowledge of the Lord. This, too, is clearly proclaimed by God through His prophet Isaiah:

And there shall come forth a rod out of the stem of Jesse, and a Branch shall grow out of his roots: and the spirit of the LORD *shall rest upon him, the spirit of wisdom and understanding, the spirit of counsel and might, the spirit of knowledge and of the fear of the* LORD; *and shall make him of quick understanding in the fear of the* LORD: *and he shall not judge after the sight of his eyes, neither reprove after the hearing of his ears: but with righteousness shall he judge the poor, and reprove with equity for the meek of the earth: and he shall smite the earth with the rod of his mouth, and with the breath of his lips shall he slay the wicked. And righteousness shall be the girdle of his loins, and faithfulness the girdle of his reins....They shall not hurt nor destroy in all my holy mountain: for the earth shall be full of the knowledge of the* LORD, *as the waters cover the sea.* (Isaiah 11:1–5, 9)

Results Regarding the Antichrist and the Devil

Next, we will see the results of our Lord's return on the Antichrist and the Devil.

The Antichrist Is Defeated

As a result of the return of our Lord Jesus, the Antichrist will be put out of the way. As the Holy Spirit said through the apostle Paul in 2 Thessalonians,

> *Let no man deceive you by any means: for that day shall not come, except there come a falling away first, and that man of sin be revealed, the son of perdition; who opposeth and exalteth himself above all that is called God, or that is worshipped; so that he as God sitteth in the temple of God, showing himself that he is God....For the mystery of iniquity doth already work: only he who now letteth* [restrains] *will let* [restrain], *until he be taken out of the way. And then shall that Wicked* [the Antichrist] *be revealed, whom the Lord shall consume* [or, put out of the way; see Revelation 19:20] *with the spirit of his mouth, and shall destroy with the brightness of his coming.*   (2 Thessalonians 2:3–4, 7–8)

It is clearly revealed in the Word of God that there is a mighty king coming to this earth, the personal representative of Satan, who will gain great power and dominion throughout the world. The days of his reign will be awful days, but they will be brief and his overthrow overwhelming.

The Devil Is Tormented Forever

The Devil himself will be chained and cast into the abyss for a thousand years, and then after a short time of liberty he will be cast into the lake of fire, where he will be tormented day and night forever and ever. This, too, is clearly revealed in God's Word:

> *And I saw an angel come down from heaven, having the key of the bottomless pit and a great chain in his hand. And he laid hold on the dragon, that old serpent, which is the Devil, and Satan, and bound him a thousand years, and cast him into the bottomless pit, and shut him up, and set a seal upon him, that he should deceive the nations no more, till the thousand years should be fulfilled: and after that he must be loosed a little season.* (Revelation 20:1–3)

In verses four through six is a brief account of the thousand years. Then we read in the next four verses,

> *And when the thousand years are expired, Satan shall be loosed out of his prison, and shall go out to deceive the nations which are in the four quarters of the earth, Gog and Magog, to gather them together to battle: the number of whom is as the sand of the sea. And they went up on the breadth of the earth, and compassed the camp of the saints about, and the beloved city: and fire came down from God out of heaven, and devoured them. And the devil that deceived them was cast into the lake of fire and brimstone, where the beast and the false prophet are, and shall be tormented day and night for ever and ever.* (Revelation 20:7–10)

Results Regarding the Physical Universe

Now we will examine the effects of our Lord's return on the physical universe. The second coming of our Lord will affect not only man, but the physical universe as well.

Creation Is Liberated

In connection with Christ's coming again and as a result of it, the creation itself will be delivered from the bondage of corruption to which it is now subject; it will enjoy the liberty of the glory of the children of God. Thorns and briars and carnage will be no more. Even the wilderness and the solitary place and the desert will rejoice and blossom as the rose. (See Isaiah 35:1.) This is revealed in both the Old Testament and the New. The apostle Paul wrote,

> *For the earnest expectation of the creature waiteth for the manifestation of the sons of God. For the creature was made subject to vanity, not willingly, but by reason of him who hath subjected the same in hope, because the creature itself also shall be delivered from the bondage of corruption into the glorious liberty of the children of God.* (Romans 8:19–21)

Everywhere in nature we find pain and suffering, disease and death. Much of the music of the insects that we hear in the air is not a song of joy but the sound of pain. But the glad day is coming when pain and disease and death will cease among the lower orders of creation as well as among men. Just as nature fell with the fall of man, who is the head of the earthly creation, nature will also be redeemed when man is redeemed. This will be fulfilled in connection with the coming of Christ. The prophet Isaiah said,

> *Instead of the thorn shall come up the fir tree, and instead of the brier shall come up the myrtle tree: and it shall be to the* LORD *for a name, for an everlasting sign that shall not be cut off.* (Isaiah 55:13)

This is not poetry and figurative speech, but the revelation of literal facts that will take place upon this earth.

Again Isaiah said,

The wolf and the lamb shall feed together, and the lion shall eat straw like the bullock: and dust shall be the serpent's meat. They shall not hurt nor destroy in all my holy mountain, saith the LORD. (Isaiah 65:25)

The carnivorous beast will be changed. Not even the wolf will destroy the lamb; they will both eat grass.

Again Isaiah said, "*The wilderness* [will] *be a fruitful field, and the fruitful field* [will] *be counted for a forest*" (Isaiah 32:15). And once more we read,

The wilderness and the solitary place shall be glad for them; and the desert shall rejoice, and blossom as the rose. It shall blossom abundantly, and rejoice even with joy and singing: the glory of Lebanon shall be given unto it, the excellency of Carmel and Sharon, they shall see the glory of the LORD, *and the excellency of our God.* (Isaiah 35:1–2)

The most desolate parts of the earth will become more beautiful and fruitful than the most fertile parts of the earth are today.

A New Heaven and a New Earth

As bright as the preceding picture is, an even better day is coming, a day in which there will be a new heaven and a new earth! We read in 2 Peter,

Seeing then that all these things shall be dissolved, what manner of persons ought ye to be in all holy conversation and godliness, looking for and hasting unto the coming of the day of God, wherein the heavens being on fire shall be dissolved, and the elements shall melt with fervent heat? Nevertheless we, according to his promise, look for new heavens and a new earth, wherein dwelleth righteousness. (2 Peter 3:11–13)

We see a picture of the fulfillment of this prophecy in the book of Revelation:

> *And I saw a new heaven and a new earth: for the first heaven and the first earth were passed away; and there was no more sea. And I John saw the holy city, new Jerusalem, coming down from God out of heaven, prepared as a bride adorned for her husband. And I heard a great voice out of heaven saying, Behold, the tabernacle of God is with men, and he will dwell with them, and they shall be his people, and God himself shall be with them, and be their God. And God shall wipe away all tears from their eyes; and there shall be no more death, neither sorrow, nor crying, neither shall there be any more pain: for the former things are passed away. And he that sat upon the throne said, Behold, I make all things new. And he said unto me, Write: for these words are true and faithful.*
>
> (Revelation 21:1–5)

To sum it all up, as the result of our Lord's return, there will be a new and glorious man, in a new and glorious body, in a new and glorious society, in a new and glorious universe. *"Amen. Even so, come, Lord Jesus"* (Revelation 22:20).

Chapter 6

WHEN IS HE COMING?

It is not for you to know the times or the seasons, which the
Father hath put in his own power.
—Acts 1:7

But, beloved, be not ignorant of this one thing,
that one day is with the Lord as a thousand years,
and a thousand years as one day.
—2 Peter 3:8

Over and over again, we are told in the Word of God that the exact time of our Lord's return is not known, and cannot be known, by man. Our Lord Jesus Himself declared in Matthew 24:36, *"But of that day and hour knoweth no man, no, not the angels of heaven, but my Father only."* And on the grounds that we do not know the exact time of our Lord's return, He said, *"Watch therefore: for ye know not what hour your Lord doth come"* (Matthew 24:42). In Mark 13:32 Jesus Christ said, *"But of that day and that hour knoweth no man, no, not the angels which are in heaven, neither the Son, but the Father."*

Many are trying to calculate the exact date of our Lord's return by using the data given in Daniel, but all such calculations are utterly unreliable. The statements in the book of Daniel were not intended to give us a clue to the exact date of Christ's return; therefore, to attempt to arrive at the date by such calculations is to attempt the impossible. It is part of God's purpose and method in dealing with men to keep them in uncertainty on this point. The things that are revealed belong to us, but this is one of *"the secret things* [that] *belong unto the* LORD *our God"* (Deuteronomy 29:29).

The prophecies of Daniel existed in the days of Jesus, and doubtless He understood the lessons those prophecies were intended to teach, but He distinctly declared that even He did not know the day or the hour of His coming again. As a man setting an example for us to follow, He had put away the knowledge of the time of this event.

After His resurrection, our Lord declared to His disciples that God did not desire for us to know the date that He would return again. His disciples had asked Him, *"Lord, wilt thou at this time restore again the kingdom to Israel?"* and He said to them, *"It is not for you to know the times or the seasons, which the Father hath put in his own power"* (Acts 1:6–7). Let us leave the times where God has put them—within His own authority. Any teacher who attempts to pinpoint the date of Christ's return is at once discredited, and it is entirely unnecessary to waste time by wading through his futile calculations.

When People Least Expect Him

While we are not told the exact time of our Lord's return, we are told that it will be at such a time as even His disciples are not expecting it. Our Lord said, *"Therefore be ye also ready: for in such an hour as ye think not the Son of man cometh"* (Matthew 24:44). It will not be a time when there is a widespread expectation of our Lord's coming; it will be a time when people do not expect Him. Even the faithful and wise servant will be surprised, though he will be found doing his Master's will:

> *Who then is a faithful and wise servant, whom his lord hath made ruler over his household, to give them meat in due*

*season? Blessed is that servant, whom his lord when he cometh
shall find so doing.* (Matthew 24:45–46)

When the World Is Preoccupied

The time of our Lord's return will be a time when the world is
absorbed in its usual occupations:

> *And as it was in the days of Noe [Noah], so shall it be also
> in the days of the Son of man. They did eat, they drank, they
> married wives, they were given in marriage, until the day that
> Noe [Noah] entered into the ark, and the flood came, and
> destroyed them all. Likewise also as it was in the days of Lot;
> they did eat, they drank, they bought, they sold, they planted,
> they builded; but the same day that Lot went out of Sodom it
> rained fire and brimstone from heaven, and destroyed them
> all. Even thus shall it be in the day when the Son of man is
> revealed.* (Luke 17:26–30)

Everything will be going on in its customary way. As already
said in another chapter, men and women will not be gathered on
hilltops in white robes waiting for the descent of their Lord. On
the contrary, people will be engrossed in their ordinary occupations—eating and drinking, marrying and being given in marriage, buying and selling, planting and building. Everything will
go on as usual up to the very moment of our Lord's coming.

Some would stretch these words further than this and make
them teach that as the days of Noah and Lot were peculiarly wicked
days, so the days of our Lord's return will be days of extraordinary
wickedness, but this is stretching the words that our Lord spoke
here beyond their evident intent. Our Lord meant what He explicitly said, that people will be engaged in their usual occupations,
little thinking the Lord is near, and in a moment He will come.

The Day of the Lord

Writing to the Thessalonians, who had been disturbed by the thought that the Day of the Lord had already come, Paul said,

> *That ye be not soon shaken in mind, or be troubled, neither by spirit, nor by word, nor by letter as from us, as that the day of Christ* [or, the Day of the Lord] *is at hand* [the Revised Version says, *"now present,"* meaning, "has actually arrived"]. *Let no man deceive you by any means: for that day shall not come, except there come a falling away first, and that man of sin be revealed, the son of perdition; who opposeth and exalteth himself above all that is called God, or that is worshipped; so that he as God sitteth in the temple of God, showing himself that he is God.*   (2 Thessalonians 2:2–4)

Paul plainly stated in these verses that the Day of the Lord will not come until after the revelation of the Man of Sin (the Antichrist). Of course, the Day of the Lord is the time of the Lord's coming to the earth. This, as we have already seen, is preceded by His coming into the air to receive His bride, the church, unto Himself. There is nothing in Scripture that shows that a period of time will not pass between the coming of Christ for His saints in the air and His coming with His saints to the earth. Indeed, there are indications that there must be such an interval. Christ has much to do with His church before He comes with them to deal with the world.

Furthermore, we are distinctly taught in this same chapter that there is now a restraining power that hinders the manifestation of the Man of Sin:

> *And now ye know what withholdeth that he might be revealed in his time. For the mystery of iniquity doth already work:*

*only he who now letteth [restrains] will let [restrain], until
he be taken out of the way. And then shall that Wicked [the
Antichrist] be revealed, whom the Lord shall consume with
the spirit of his mouth, and shall destroy with the brightness of
his coming.* (2 Thessalonians 2:6–8)

It is only natural to presume that this restraining power has
something to do with the church; and the inevitable implication
seems to be that the church must be removed from the earth before
that Wicked One can be revealed on the earth.

Perilous Times of Apostasy

The last days and the time of our Lord's return will be a time of
apostasy. We read in 1 Timothy, *"Now the Spirit speaketh expressly,
that in the latter times some shall depart from the faith, giving heed to
seducing spirits, and doctrines of devils"* (1 Timothy 4:1). By *"doctrines of devils,"* Paul evidently meant the teachings that evil spirits
will spread through men and women who are under their control,
such as the teaching of spiritualism, the belief that we can communicate with the dead, which might more properly be termed
"demonism." The astounding growth of belief in the occult in our
day seems to be a fulfillment of this word of prophesy. On every
hand, people seem to be departing from *"the faith which was once
delivered unto the saints"* (Jude 1:3) and giving heed to all kinds of
evil spirits.

We are further told by Paul that the last days will be *"perilous
times."* He said,

*This know also, that in the last days perilous times shall come.
For men shall be lovers of their own selves, covetous, boasters, proud, blasphemers, disobedient to parents, unthankful, unholy, without natural affection, trucebreakers, false*

accusers, incontinent, fierce, despisers of those that are good, traitors, heady, highminded, lovers of pleasures more than lovers of God; having a form of godliness, but denying the power thereof.   (2 Timothy 3:1–5)

These words present to us a remarkably accurate picture of our own time. If we were to examine in detail each item in Paul's description of the last days, we would find them amazingly fulfilled in our own time. This naturally leads many to suppose that the Lord's coming is very near at hand. However, we should always bear in mind that students of the Bible and earnest men of God have often thought in the past that the coming of the Lord was very near. Martin Luther, for example, thought this centuries ago. These men of the past were not mistaken. The return of our Lord was very near. Those who were mistaken were those who thought it to be so far away that they let it have no effect on their lives.

At the present time, we see the following signs of His coming, which may take place very soon: the numerous iniquities of our day; the apostasy into damning error and unbelief on the part of many professed Christians who had appeared to be sincere; the apostasy of many professedly evangelical preachers; the apostasy of many theological professors in seminaries that were founded and built at great sacrifice by orthodox men and women for the dissemination of truth and not for the breeding of error; the increase of lawlessness on the part of great corporations on the one hand, and on the part of the oppressed poor on the other hand; the mutterings that precede a storm of wild anarchy, which seems likely to break soon.

"Men's hearts [are] failing them for fear, and for looking after those things which are coming on the earth" (Luke 21:26). Many of the greatest statesmen of England, America, and Germany have forebodings that they scarcely dare to put into words of what lies just a little way ahead for the nations of the earth. But in such days

as these, our hearts should not faint or fear. *"When these things begin to come to pass, then look up, and lift up your heads; for your redemption draweth nigh"* (Luke 21:28). The darker the day grows, the closer the dawn is; and just at the moment when things seem unendurable, the brightest, gladdest day the earth has ever seen will dawn.

At Any Moment

The return of our Lord is an event that, as far as we know, may occur at any moment. We are repeatedly exhorted in the Bible to be watching, looking, and prepared for our Lord's return. In the book of Mark, our Lord Jesus said to His disciples,

For the Son of man is as a man taking a far journey, who left his house, and gave authority to his servants, and to every man his work, and commanded the porter to watch. Watch ye therefore: for ye know not when the master of the house cometh, at even [evening], *or at midnight, or at the cockcrowing, or in the morning: lest coming suddenly he find you sleeping.* (Mark 13:34–36)

Again, in the book of Luke, our Lord is recorded as saying,

Let your loins be girded about [keep yourself dressed and ready]*, and your lights burning; and ye yourselves like unto men that wait for their lord, when he will return from the wedding; that when he cometh and knocketh, they may open unto him immediately.* (Luke 12:35–36)

Still again, we read in Matthew 25:13 these words of our Lord: *"Watch therefore, for ye know neither the day nor the hour."* In the preceding chapter, we read, *"Watch therefore: for ye know not what hour your Lord doth come.…Therefore be ye also ready: for in such an hour as ye think not the Son of man cometh"* (Matthew 24:42, 44).

If we knew that there were any event, or series of events, that must occur before our Lord comes to receive His own unto Himself, we could not be watching as our Lord bids us to watch in these passages. I was once talking with a friend who believed that the Tribulation must come before our Lord could come, and I asked him how we could be watching and looking for our Lord if we knew that He could not come for some years yet, namely until after the Tribulation had occurred. He replied that there was "no psychological difficulty at all." But there *is* a psychological difficulty. It is an absolute impossibility for an intelligent man to be watching for an event that he knows cannot occur for some years.

So it is evident from the clear teaching of Jesus Himself that His coming is an event that, as far as we know, may occur at any moment. There is no event or series of events predicted in Scripture that must occur before our Lord Jesus comes to receive His own unto Himself. It is true there are events that must occur before He comes to the earth with His saints (see 2 Thessalonians 2:1–4), but He may come for us, as far as we know, at any moment. It is important to be always ready, "*for in such an hour as ye think not the Son of man cometh*" (Matthew 24:44).

But some people say, "Will the world not be converted before Jesus Christ comes?" The simplest way to answer this question is to read the Bible's descriptions of the state of affairs when our Lord comes again. We read, for example, in Revelation 1:7, "*Behold, he cometh with clouds; and every eye shall see him, and they also which pierced him: and all kindreds of the earth shall wail because of him.*" This certainly does not picture a converted world, not a world rejoicing at the return of their Lord, but all the tribes of the earth mourning. Even more explicitly, if that is possible, we read in the book of Matthew,

> *When the Son of man shall come in his glory, and all the holy angels with him, then shall he sit upon the throne of his glory:*

and before him shall be gathered all nations: and he shall sepa-
rate them one from another, as a shepherd divideth his sheep
from the goats. (Matthew 25:31–32)

This passage certainly does not portray the whole world as converted.

Still again we read,

That ye be not soon shaken in mind, or be troubled, neither
by spirit, nor by word, nor by letter as from us, as that the day
of Christ is at hand. Let no man deceive you by any means:
for that day shall not come, except there come a falling away
first, and that man of sin be revealed, the son of perdition; who
opposeth and exalteth himself above all that is called God, or
that is worshipped; so that he as God sitteth in the temple of
God, showing himself that he is God....And then shall that
Wicked be revealed, whom the Lord shall consume with the
spirit of his mouth, and shall destroy with the brightness of his
coming. (2 Thessalonians 2:2–4, 8)

This depicts anything but a converted world at the time of our Lord's return.

Our Lord Himself on one occasion said, "*Nevertheless when the Son of man cometh, shall he find faith on the earth?*" (Luke 18:8). The clear implication of these words is that when the Lord comes, far from the whole world being converted, real faith will be a difficult thing to find. The Lord said again,

And take heed to yourselves, lest at any time your hearts be
overcharged with surfeiting [overindulgence]*, and drunken-*
ness, and cares of this life, and so that day come upon you
unawares. For as a snare shall it come on all them that dwell
on the face of the whole earth. (Luke 21:34–35)

This certainly does not present to us a world already converted at the time of our Lord's return.

The Holy Spirit spoke the same thing through the apostle Paul:

> *This know also, that in the last days perilous times shall come. For men shall be lovers of their own selves, covetous, boasters, proud, blasphemers, disobedient to parents, unthankful, unholy, without natural affection, trucebreakers, false accusers, incontinent, fierce, despisers of those that are good, traitors, heady, highminded, lovers of pleasures more than lovers of God; having a form of godliness, but denying the power thereof: from such turn away.*   (2 Timothy 3:1–5)

These verses do not describe a converted world, but a world just as we see it today.

There will be two classes, converted and unconverted, at the revelation of Jesus Christ from heaven. The apostle Paul said,

> *Seeing it is a righteous thing with God to recompense tribulation to them that trouble you; and to you who are troubled rest with us, when the Lord Jesus shall be revealed from heaven with his mighty angels, in flaming fire taking vengeance on them that know not God, and that obey not the gospel of our Lord Jesus Christ: who shall be punished with everlasting destruction from the presence of the Lord, and from the glory of his power; when he shall come to be glorified in his saints, and to be admired in all them that believe (because our testimony among you was believed) in that day.*
>
> (2 Thessalonians 1:6–10)

It is perfectly evident from all these passages that the whole world will not be converted before the return of our Lord. "But," some people ask, "how will you explain Matthew 24:14: 'And this *gospel of the kingdom shall be preached in all the world for a witness unto all nations; and then shall the end come'?* Does this not predict a converted world at the coming of the Lord?" It certainly does not. This verse can be explained by simply noticing what it says.

First of all, this verse tells us that the Gospel is to be preached *"for a witness"* to all the nations, not that all the nations will be converted. The Gospel has certainly been preached throughout the United States, but no intelligent person would claim that all Americans are converted.

In the second place, in a sense, and in a scriptural sense, too, the Gospel has already been preached for a testimony to the ends of the world. Paul could say even in his day, *"But I say, Have they not heard? Yes verily, their sound went into all the earth, and their words unto the ends of the world"* (Romans 10:18). He could further say, *"The hope of the gospel, which ye have heard, and which was preached to every creature which is under heaven"* (Colossians 1:23).

In the third place, Matthew 24:14 tells us that the Gospel of the kingdom will be preached in all the world, and *"then shall the end come."* The coming of Jesus Christ to receive His own is not the end; it is but the beginning of the end. Therefore, Christ could come before the Gospel has been preached in the whole world.

But some people ask, "If the Lord Jesus may come at any moment, how can we explain 2 Thessalonians 2:2–4?" These verses state,

> *That ye be not soon shaken in mind, or be troubled, neither by spirit, nor by word, nor by letter as from us, as that the day of Christ [or, the Day of the Lord] is at hand. Let no man deceive you by any means: for that day shall not come, except there come a falling away first, and that man of sin be revealed, the son of perdition; who opposeth and exalteth himself above all that is called God, or that is worshipped; so that*

> he as God sitteth in the temple of God, showing himself that he
> is God.   (2 Thessalonians 2:2–4)

The answer to this is very simple. It is true that the Man of Sin must be revealed before the Day of the Lord comes. However, the Day of the Lord is not the coming of Christ to receive His church, but that which follows it. How closely it may follow it is difficult for us to say. The Thessalonians were troubled by the teaching that had risen among them that the Day of the Lord was already present, and that they were in the midst of judgment. They were greatly agitated and perturbed by this teaching. Paul showed them that this could not be possible, for the *"man of sin,"* who was to be especially dealt with in the Day of the Lord, had not yet been revealed.

Important Questions

At this point the question arises, Will the church go through the Great Tribulation? In answer to this I would say that it is clear from the Bible that the church will pass through tribulation and troubles. Paul and Barnabas taught the disciples in Lystra and Iconium and Antioch *"that we must through much tribulation enter into the kingdom of God"* (Acts 14:22). But to say that the church will pass through tribulation, or even much tribulation, is not at all to say that the church will pass through the Great Tribulation. In the Great Tribulation, God deals with a Christ-rejecting world. The Great Tribulation has to do with the Jews primarily, not the Gentiles. The whole book of Revelation after Revelation 4:1 has to do with the time after the rapture of the church. There is much to indicate that the church will be shielded during this period. Of course, by the church we mean the true church, all those who are united to Jesus Christ by a living faith. In connection with a passage about the Great Tribulation, our Lord said,

Watch ye therefore, and pray always, that ye may be accounted worthy to escape all these things that shall come to pass, and to stand before the Son of man. (Luke 21:36)

There is one other question that arises at this point: Is the world getting better? To answer this question intelligently we must ask, What is meant by "the world"? If you use "the world" in the biblical sense, it certainly cannot be getting better, for we are taught distinctly in 1 John 5:19 that *"the whole world lieth in wickedness."* In biblical usage, the world is the whole body of men and women who reject Christ. It *"lieth in wickedness,"* and certainly in such an embrace it cannot be getting better. Furthermore, the Devil is its god. The apostle Paul said,

In whom the god of this world hath blinded the minds of them which believe not, lest the light of the glorious gospel of Christ, who is the image of God, should shine unto them. (2 Corinthians 4:4)

The world is, of course, necessarily growing worse.

But if we mean by "the world"—as men usually do when they ask this question—the entire mass of people, Christians and non-Christians, that makes up present human society, then it is to be said there are two developments going on side by side at the present time—the development of the kingdom of God and the development of the kingdom of Satan. These two developments will be brought to a crisis when the Antichrist appears at the head of Satan's kingdom and Christ appears at the head of God's kingdom. The crisis will end in a complete victory for Christ and the kingdom of God.

In the meantime, God is gathering out of the world a people for His name. As James put it in Acts 15:14, *"God...did visit the Gentiles, to take out of them a people for his name."* The purpose of the preaching of the Gospel of grace in this present dispensation is not the winning of the whole world for Christ, but the gathering out of the world a people for His name. Many people in these days raise the cry, "America for Christ," or, "The whole wide world for Christ." But those who know their Bibles know that we will not see "America for Christ" or "The whole wide world for Christ" in the present dispensation. The Gospel of grace has not failed; it is accomplishing just what God intended it to accomplish: the gathering out of the world a people for His name, that is, the church, the bride of Christ. Those whom God is gathering out of the world as a people for His name are growing in the knowledge and likeness of Him, and the world is of necessity influenced by them to a certain extent. The influence of Christianity is seen in the political, commercial, and social life of the day, and in that sense the world might be said to be growing better.

On the other hand, every person whose eyes are open to what is going on in the world today must see that there is what Scripture predicted there would be: the development of *"the mystery of iniquity"* (2 Thessalonians 2:7). There is, it is true, some restraining power at present, but nevertheless *"the mystery of iniquity doth already work"* (verse 7). Some of the results of this wicked work are as follows: increasing error and apostasy in the professing church, as well as out of it; growing immorality (for example, along the lines of divorce, impurity, and immodesty in dress); and especially the development of anarchy, or lawlessness, among all classes of society. In this sense, the world is growing worse.

However, we should not be at all disheartened by this fact; it is a fulfillment of prophecy. Indeed, the darkest clouds that are gathering are but harbingers of the golden day that is coming when our Lord Himself will return and take up the reins of government.

Chapter 7

READY OR NOT

The grace of God that bringeth salvation hath appeared to all men, teaching us that, denying ungodliness and worldly lusts, we should live soberly, righteously, and godly, in this present world; looking for that blessed hope, and the glorious appearing of the great God and our Saviour Jesus Christ.
—Titus 2:11–13

The all-important, practical question for each of us in connection with our Lord's return is, What should be my personal attitude toward His coming again? This question is specifically answered in the Bible. The Bible's treatment of the doctrine of Christ's second coming is intensely practical.

Ready for His Return

In the first place, we should be ready for our Lord's return regardless of when He comes. We should faithfully obey our Lord's own commandment: *"Be ye also ready: for in such an hour as ye think not the Son of man cometh"* (Matthew 24:44). We should not only listen to these words, but we should keep them in mind every day of our lives. Every morning when we rise we should say to ourselves, "Be ready for your Lord's return, for He may come today." Every night before we lie down to sleep, we should ask ourselves, "Would I be ready for my Lord's return if He should come before I wake in the morning?" The imminent return of our Lord is the great biblical motivation for a pure, unselfish, devoted, unworldly, active life of service. In much of our modern preaching, we urge people to live righteously and work diligently because death is swiftly coming, but this is never the scriptural rationale. The Bible argument always is, "Christ is coming. Be ready when He comes." This leads inevitably to the question, What constitutes readiness for the coming of Christ?

The book of Luke answers the question:

> *And take heed to yourselves, lest at any time your hearts be overcharged with surfeiting* [overindulgence], *and drunkenness, and cares of this life, and so that day come upon you unawares. For as a snare shall it come on all them that dwell on the face of the whole earth. Watch ye therefore, and pray always, that ye may be accounted worthy to escape all these things that shall come to pass, and to stand before the Son of man.* (Luke 21:34–36)

In other words, separation from the world's indulgence of the flesh, separation from the world's immersion in the affairs of this life, and intense earnestness in daily prayer constitute the first part of preparation for the Lord's return. There are many who abstain from alcohol who, nevertheless, live for their bellies; Paul's simple but impressive way of putting it is, "*Whose God is their belly*" (Philippians 3:19). They do not eat for strength for service, but for gratification of appetite; they even eat what they know is harmful. There are others who live very frugally but who are completely sunken in worldly cares. And there are still others who are very active in Christian service but who are neglectful of prayer. They do not "*watch…and pray always*" (Luke 21:36). None of these are ready for the Master's coming.

In the two parables concerning our Lord's return in Matthew 25:1–30, we see that having oil in our vessels—that is, receiving continuous supplies of the Holy Spirit—and being faithful in the use of our talents in our Lord's service are two all-important factors in readiness for our Lord's return. I would ask every reader of this book, "Have you received the Holy Spirit, and are you constantly receiving fresh supplies of His presence and power?" And I would ask you again, "Are you diligently using for Him all the talents that our Lord Jesus has confided to you?" If you fail at either point, you are not ready for our Lord's return.

In 1 John 2:28 we read, "*And now, little children, abide in him; that, when he shall appear, we may have confidence, and not be ashamed before him at his coming.*" Here we find that abiding in Him constitutes readiness for Him when He comes. Are you abiding in Him? Have you truly renounced your own wisdom, your own strength, and your own life; and are you daily and hourly just looking to Him for His wisdom and His strength and His life?

Watching for His Return

In the second place, we should be watching for the coming of our Lord. Our Lord Himself said,

> *And ye yourselves like unto men that wait for their lord, when he will return from the wedding; that when he cometh and knocketh, they may open unto him immediately. Blessed are those servants, whom the lord when he cometh shall find watching.* (Luke 12:36–37)

It is not enough that our lives are right and our service earnest; we should be alert and should expect the coming of the Lord. A special blessing is here pronounced upon those servants who are watching for the Lord's return: "*Verily I say unto you, that he shall gird himself, and make them to sit down to meat, and will come forth and serve them"* (Luke 12:37). Would that blessing be yours if He should come today? Would He find you watching? Oh, let us be watching and expectant and living every hour with the thought of His coming! Never do anything that you would not gladly have Him find you doing if He should come. Never leave anything undone that you would wish that you had done if He should come. Never go any place where you would not be glad to have Him find you if He should come.

Longing for His Return

However, it is not enough to be ready and watching for the Lord's return. We should earnestly desire the coming of our Lord. Peter wrote,

> *Looking for and hasting unto* [earnestly desiring] *the coming of the day of God, wherein the heavens being on fire shall be dissolved, and the elements shall melt with fervent heat.*
> (2 Peter 3:12)

If we love our Lord above all else, we will long for His return above all else. How a loving wife longs for the return of her husband who is across the sea. Just as no gift that he can send her will compensate for his absence, so the true bride of Christ longs for the return of the heavenly Bridegroom. While she may rejoice in the grace given her in the present through the indwelling Christ, she longs for the return of the Bridegroom Himself.

I once heard a widely acclaimed teacher say that there was a time when he was greatly interested in the second coming of Christ, but that in recent years he had been so taken up with the glory of the indwelling Christ that he had lost interest in the thought of His return. This statement is thoroughly unscriptural. To me it is incomprehensible how someone who really knows the truth about the return of our Lord could say this. It is worthwhile to preach the present privileges of the indwelling Christ, but there is something better than even this. Our Lord Himself is coming! We will see Him! We will be caught up to meet Him! We will forever be with Him! And if it is He whom we love, and not merely His gifts, no joy and victory that we may know through the indwelling Christ will satisfy the deepest longings of our soul. We will long for Him and for that fullness of fellowship with Him that we will know only when He Himself comes again.

There is a crown awaiting those who *"love his appearing"* (2 Timothy 4:8). It is doubtful that there was ever a believer on this earth who knew more experientially about the glory of the indwelling Christ than the apostle Paul, yet one of the last things he wrote was this:

Henceforth there is laid up for me a crown of righteousness, which the Lord, the righteous judge, shall give me at that day: and not to me only, but unto all them also that love his appearing. (2 Timothy 4:8)

May I be straightforward and ask you a question? Are you longing for Christ's return? If you are not, you may be sure there is something wrong somewhere in your life or in your relationship with your Lord.

Our Lord Jesus is coming again—precious words! How they ought to thrill our hearts! How they do thrill our hearts! How they ought to lead us to inquire diligently lest there be anything in us that would grieve Him at His coming. How they ought to make our hearts burn with the desire to do more and to use our talents more faithfully while He tarries.

The Lord Jesus is coming! How small these words make the world seem with its gain and its loss, its pride and its humiliation, its pleasure and its pain, its praise and its blame. Our Lord Jesus is coming! How these words should make us eager to bring our friends to Christ at once lest they be left behind at His coming. Our Lord Jesus is coming! Yes, He is coming—perhaps this year, perhaps this month, perhaps tomorrow, perhaps today. Are you ready? Listen once again to His last and sweetest promise: *"Surely I come quickly"* (Revelation 22:20). May we earnestly reply, *"Amen. Even so, come, Lord Jesus"* (verse 20).

ABOUT THE AUTHOR

Reuben Archer Torrey (1856–1928) was born in Hoboken, New Jersey, on January 28, 1856. He graduated from Yale University in 1875 and from Yale Divinity School in 1878.

Upon his graduation, Dr. Torrey became a Congregational minister. A few years later, he joined Dwight L. Moody in his evangelistic work in Chicago and became the pastor of the Chicago Avenue Church. He was selected by D. L. Moody to become the first dean of the Moody Bible Institute of Chicago. Under his direction, Moody Institute became a pattern for Bible institutes around the world.

Torrey is respected as one of the greatest evangelists of modern times. At the turn of the century, he began his evangelistic tours and crusades. He spent the years of 1903–1905 in a worldwide revival campaign, along with the famous song leader Charles McCallon Alexander. Together they ministered in many parts of the world and reportedly brought nearly one hundred thousand souls to Jesus. Torrey continued worldwide crusades for the next fifteen years, eventually reaching Japan and China. During those same years, he served as Dean of the Bible Institute of Los Angeles and pastored the Church of the Open Door in that city.

Torrey longed for more Christian workers to take an active part in bringing the message of salvation through Christ to a lost and dying world. His straightforward style of evangelism has shown thousands of Christian workers how to become effective soulwinners.

Dr. Torrey died on October 26, 1928. He is well remembered today for his inspiring devotional books on the Christian life, which have been translated into many different languages. Woven throughout his many books, the evangelistic message that sent Torrey around the world still ministers to all whose hearts yearn to lead men, women, and children to salvation through Jesus Christ.